GEORGIAN POETRY

Published November 1919

GEORGIAN POETRY

POETRY

1918-1919

SEVENTH THOUSAND

THE POETRY BOOKSHOP
35 Devonshire Street
Theobalds Road
W.C.1
MCMXX

TO

THOMAS HARDY

PREFATORY NOTE

THIS is the fourth volume of the present series. I hope it may be thought to show that what for want of a better word is called Peace has not interfered with the writing of good poetry.

Thanks and acknowledgements are due to Messrs. Beaumont, Blackwell, Collins, Constable, Fifield, Heinemann, Secker, Selwyn & Blount, and Sidgwick & Jackson ; and to the Editors of *The Anglo-French Review, The Athenaeum, The Chapbook, Land and Water, The Nation, The New Statesman, The New Witness, The New World, The Owl, The Spectator, To-day, Voices,* and *The Westminster Gazette.*

E. M.

September, 1919.

CONTENTS

LASCELLES ABERCROMBIE

WITCHCRAFT: NEW STYLE

Lascelles
Abercrombie

The sun drew off at last his piercing fires.
Over the stale warm air, dull as a pond
And moveless in the grey quieted street,
Blue magic of a summer evening glowed.
The sky, that had been dazzling stone all day,
Hollowed in smooth hard brightness, now dissolved
To infinite soft depth, and smoulder'd down
Low as the roofs, dark burning blue, and soared
Clear to that winking drop of liquid silver,
The first exquisite star. Now the half-light
Tidied away the dusty litter parching
Among the cobbles, veiled in the colour of distance
Shabby slates and brickwork mouldering, turn'd
The hunchback houses into patient things
Resting ; and golden windows now began.

A little brisk grey slattern of a woman,
Pattering along in her loose-heel'd clogs,
Pusht the brass-barr'd door of a public-house ;
The spring went hard against her ; hand and knee
Shoved their weak best. As the door poised ajar,
Hullabaloo of talking men burst out,
A pouring babble of inflamed palaver,
And overriding it and shouted down
High words, jeering or downright, broken like
Crests that leap and stumble in rushing water.
Just as the door went wide and she stept in,
' She cannot do it ! ' one was bawling out :
A glaring hulk of flesh with a bull's voice.
He finger'd with his neckerchief, and stretcht
His throat to ease the anger of dispute,
Then spat to put a full stop to the matter.

3

Lascelles	The little woman waited, with one hand
Abercrombie	Propping the door, and smiled at the loud man.

They saw her then ; and the sight was enough
To gag the speech of every drinker there :
The din fell down like something chopt off short.
Blank they all wheel'd towards her, with their mouths
Still gaping as though full of voiceless words.
She let the door slam to ; and all at ease,
Amused, her smile wrinkling about her eyes,
Went forward : they made room for her quick enough.
Her chin just topt the counter ; she gave in
Her bottle to the potboy, tuckt it back,
Full of bright tawny ale, under her arm,
Rapt down the coppers on the planisht zinc,
And turned : and no word spoken all the while.

    The first voice, in that silent crowd, was hers,
Her light snickering laugh, as she stood there
Pausing, scanning the sawdust at her feet.
Then she switcht round and faced the positive man
Whose strong ' She cannot do it ! ' all still felt
Huskily shouting in their guilty ears.

    ' She can't, eh ? She can't do it ? '—Then she'd
      heard !
The man, inside his ruddy insolent flesh,
Had hoped she did not hear. His barrel chest
Gave a slight cringe, as though the glint of her eyes
Prickt him. But he stood up to her awkwardly bold,
One elbow on the counter, gripping his mug
Like a man holding on to a post for safety.

The Man	You can't do what's not nature : nobody can.
The Woman	And louts like you have nature in your pocket ?
The Man	I don't say that—
The Woman	If you kept saying naught,

No one would guess the fool you are.

4

Second Man
    My very words !
The Woman   O you're the knowing man !
    The spark among the cinders !
First Man   You can't fetch
    A free man back, unless he wants to come,
The Woman Nay, I'll be bound he doesn't want to come !
Third Man And he won't come : he told me flat he wouldn't.
The Woman Are you there too ?
Third Man   And if he does come back
    It will be devilry brought him.
The Woman   I shall bring him ;—
    To-night.
First Man   How will he come ?
The Woman   Running : unless
    He's broke his leg, and then he'll have to come
    Crawling : but he will come.
First Man   How do you know
    What he may choose to do, three counties off ?
The Woman He choose ?
Third Man   You haven't got him on a lead.
The Woman Haven't I though !
Second Man   That's right ; it's what I said.
The Woman Ay, there are brains in your family.
First Man   You have
    Some sort of pull on him, to draw him home ?
The Woman You may say that : I have hold of his mind.
    And I can slack it off or fetch it taut,
    And make him dance a score of miles away
    An answer to the least twangling thrum
    I play on it. He thought he lurkt at last
    Safely ; and all the while, what has he been ?
    An eel on the end of a night line ; and it's time
    I haul'd him in. You'll see, to-night I'll land him.

Third Man	Bragging's a light job.
The Woman	You daren't let me take

Your eyes in mine !—Haul, did I say ? no need :
I give his mind a twitch, and up he comes
Tumbling home to me. Whatever work he's at,
He drops the thing he holds like redhot iron
And runs—runs till he falls down like a beast
Pole-axt, and grunts for breath ; then up and on,
No matter does he know the road or not :
The strain I put on his mind will keep him going
Right as a homing-pigeon.

First Man   Devilry
I call it.

The Woman   And you're welcome.

Second Man   But the law
Should have a say here.

The Woman   What, isn't he mine,
My own ? There's naught but what I please about it.

Third Man Why did you let him go ?

The Woman   To fetch him back !
For I enjoy this, mind. There's many a one
Would think, to see me, There goes misery !
There's a queer starveling for you !—and I do
A thing that makes me like a saint in glory,
The life of me the sound of a great tune
Your flesh could never hear : I can send power
Delighting out of me ! O, the mere thought
Has made my blood go smarting in my veins,
Such a flame glowing along it !—And all the same
I'll pay him out for sidling off from me.
But I'll have supper first.

When she was gone,   Lascelles
Their talk could scarcely raise itself again   Abercrombie
Above a grumble. But at last a cry
Sharp-pitcht came startling in from the street : at once
Their moody talk exploded into flare
Of swearing hubbub, like gunpowder dropt
On embers ; mugs were clapt down, out they bolted
Rowdily jostling, eager for the event.

All down the street the folk throng'd out of doors,
But left a narrow track clear in the middle ;
And there a man came running, a tall man
Running desperately and slowly, pounding
Like a machine, so evenly, so blindly ;
And regularly his trotting body wagg'd.
Only one foot clatter'd upon the stones ;
The other padded in his dogged stride :
The boot was gone, the sock hung frayed in shreds
About his ankle, the foot was blood and earth ;
And never a limp, not the least flinch, to tell
The wounded pulp hit stone at every step.
His clothes were tatter'd and his rent skin showed,
Harrowed with thorns. His face was pale as putty,
Thrown far back ; clots of drooping spittle foamed
On his moustache, and his hair hung in tails,
Mired with sweat ; and sightless in their sockets
His eyeballs turned up white, as dull as pebbles.
Evenly and doggedly he trotted,
And as he went he moaned. Then out of sight
Round a corner he swerved, and out of hearing.

—' The law should have a say to that, by God ! '

7

Photo by E. O. Hoppé.

John Buchan.

what I mean".

the neurotic, not the
egotism and the pride
fat and kicked. But
ants to destroy and
of the ascetic, which
of the madman that
vilisation to a feature-
to save the souls of
the inanimate corpse

n in a genial lecture
ntrymen. It was as
ted, but it had the
drew most laughter
audience where the
such spiriting ought
why Mr. Buchan
iction with his lance
this view of shorter
ndureth,'' and '' The
rocession of historic
nigration of the hero-
y amount to repeat-
praise of the delicate
he rare idealism that
No room remains

tion, and might be
laying down unnece
profoundly to literat
its extravagances a
we set visionary ch
on a level with real
more than hold their
the heir of the divi
to create a godlike
the mind are capab
than do the human
or exalted. Who o
thought of the Spar
through the monast
masterpieces on the
immortals, we or th

I have said noth
as a poet—from th
in '' The Moon En
in '' Musa Piscatrix
My preference amo
my favourite amon
gallant Montrose.
crowded career, tha
devoted to whatev
Christian chivalry

GORDON BOTTOMLEY

LITTLEHOLME

Gordon
Bottomley

(To J. S. and A. W. S.)

In entering the town, where the bright river
Shrinks in its white stone bed, old thoughts return
Of how a quiet queen was nurtured here
In the pale, shadowed ruin on the height ;
Of how, when the hoar town was new and clean
And had not grown a part of the gaunt fells
That peered down into it, the burghers wove
On their small, fireside looms green, famous webs
To cling on lissome, tower-dwelling ladies
Who rode the hills swaying like green saplings,
Or mask tall, hardy outlaws from pursuit
Down beechen caverns and green under-lights,
(The rude, vain looms are gone, their beams are broken;
Their webs are now not seen, but memory
Still tangles in their mesh the dews they swept
Like ruby sparks, the lights they took, the scents
They held, the movement of their shapes and shades) ;
Of how the Border burners in cold dawns
Of Summer hurried North up the high vales
Past smoking farmsteads that had lit the night
And surf of crowding cattle ; and of how
A laughing prince of cursed, impossible hopes
Rode through the little streets Northward to battle
And to defeat, to be a fading thought,
Belated in dead mountains of romance.

A carver at his bench in a high gable
Hears the sharp stream close under, far below
Tinkle and rustle, and no other sound
Arises there to him to change his thoughts

11

Of the changed, silent town and the dead hands
That made it and maintained it, and the need
For handiwork and happy work and work
To use and ease the mind if such sweet towns
Are to be built again or live again.

The long town ends at Littleholme, where the road
Creeps up to hills of ancient-looking stone.
Under the hanging eaves at Littleholme
A latticed casement peeps above still gardens
Into a crown of druid-solemn trees
Upon a knoll as high as a small house,
A shapely mound made so by nameless men
Whose smoothing touch yet shows through the green
hide.
When the slow moonlight drips from leaf to leaf
Of that sharp, plumy gloom, and the hour comes
When something seems awaited, though unknown,
There should appear between those leaf-thatched piles
Fresh, long-limbed women striding easily,
And men whose hair-plaits swing with their shagged
arms ;
Returning in that equal, echoed light
Which does not measure time to the dear garths
That were their own when from white Norway coasts
They landed on a kind, not distant shore,
And to the place where they have left their clothing,
Their long-accustomed bones and hair and beds
That once were pleasant to them, in that barrow
Their vanished children heaped above them dead :
For in the soundless stillness of hot noon
The mind of man, noticeable in that knoll,
Enhances its dark presence with a life
More vivid and more actual than the life

Of self-sown trees and untouched earth. It is seen   Gordon
What aspect this land had in those first eyes :   Bottomley
In that regard the works of later men
Fall in and sink like lime when it is slaked,
Staid, youthful queen and weavers are unborn,
And the new crags the Northmen saw are set
About an earth that has not been misused.

FRANCIS BRETT YOUNG

INVOCATION

Francis
Brett
Young

Whither, O, my sweet mistress, must I follow thee ?
  For when I hear thy distant footfall nearing,
  And wait on thy appearing,
Lo ! my lips are silent : no words come to me.

Once I waylaid thee in green forest covers,
  Hoping that spring might free my lips with gentle
  Alas ! her presence lingers   [fingers ;
No longer than on the plain the shadow of brown kestrel
    hovers.

Through windless ways of the night my spirit followed
    after ;—
  Cold and remote were they, and there, possessed
  By a strange unworldly rest,
Awaiting thy still voice heard only starry laughter.

The pillared halls of sleep echoed my ghostly tread.
  Yet when their secret chambers I essayed
  My spirit sank, dismayed,
Waking in fear to find the new-born vision fled.

Once indeed—but then my spirit bloomed in leafy
    rapture—
  I loved ; and once I looked death in the eyes :
  So, suddenly made wise,
Spoke of such beauty as I may never recapture. . . .

Whither, O, divine mistress, must I then follow thee ?
  Is it only in love . . . say, is it only in death
  That the spirit blossometh,
And words that may match my vision shall come to me ?

Francis
Brett
Young

When the evening came my love said to me :
 Let us go into the garden now that the sky is cool ;
The garden of black hellebore and rosemary,
 Where wild woodruff spills in a milky pool.

Low we passed in the twilight, for the wavering heat
 Of day had waned ; and round that shaded plot
Of secret beauty the thickets clustered sweet :
 Here is heaven, our hearts whispered, but our lips
  spake not.

Between that old garden and seas of lazy foam
 Gloomy and beautiful alleys of trees arise
With spire of cypress and dreamy beechen dome,
 So dark that our enchanted sight knew nothing but
  the skies :

Veiled with a soft air, drench'd in the roses' musk
 Or the dusky, dark carnation's breath of clove :
No stars burned in their deeps, but through the dusk
 I saw my love's eyes, and they were brimmed with
  love.

No star their secret ravished, no wasting moon
 Mocked the sad transience of those eternal hours :
Only the soft, unseeing heaven of June,
 The ghosts of great trees, and the sleeping flowers.

For doves that crooned in the leafy noonday now
 Were silent ; the night-jar sought his secret covers,
Nor even a mild sea-whisper moved a creaking bough—
 Was ever a silence deeper made for lovers ?

Was ever a moment meeter made for love ?   Francis
   Beautiful are your closed lips beneath my kiss ;   Brett
And all your yielding sweetness beautiful—   Young
   Oh, never in all the world was such a night as this !

Francis
Brett
Young

The robin on my lawn
He was the first to tell
How, in the frozen dawn,
This miracle befell,
Waking the meadows white
With hoar, the iron road
Agleam with splintered light,
And ice where water flowed :
Till, when the low sun drank
Those milky mists that cloak
Hanger and hollied bank,
The winter world awoke
To hear the feeble bleat
Of lambs on downland farms :
A blackbird whistled sweet ;
Old beeches moved their arms
Into a mellow haze
Aerial, newly-born :
And I, alone, agaze,
Stood waiting for the thorn
To break in blossom white,
Or burst in a green flame. . . .
So, in a single night,
Fair February came,
Bidding my lips to sing
Or whisper their surprise,
With all the joy of spring
And morning in her eyes.

LOCHANILAUN

Francis
Brett
Young

This is the image of my last content :
My soul shall be a little lonely lake,
So hidden that no shadow of man may break
The folding of its mountain battlement ;
Only the beautiful and innocent
Whiteness of sea-born cloud drooping to shake
Cool rain upon the reed-beds, or the wake
Of churn'd cloud in a howling wind's descent.
For there shall be no terror in the night
When stars that I have loved are born in me,
And cloudy darkness I will hold most fair ;
But this shall be the end of my delight :
That you, my lovely one, may stoop and see
Your image in the mirrored beauty there,

Francis
Brett
Young

LETTERMORE

These winter days on Lettermore
The brown west wind it sweeps the bay,
And icy rain beats on the bare
Unhomely fields that perish there :
The stony fields of Lettermore
That drink the white Atlantic spray.

And men who starve on Lettermore,
Cursing the haggard, hungry surf,
Will souse the autumn's bruiséd grains
To light dark fires within their brains
And fight with stones on Lettermore
Or sprawl beside the smoky turf.

When spring blows over Lettermore
To bloom the ragged furze with gold,
The lovely south wind's living breath
Is laden with the smell of death :
For fever breeds on Lettermore
To waste the eyes of young and old.

A black van comes to Lettermore ;
The horses stumble on the stones,
The drivers curse,—for it is hard
To cross the hills from Oughterard
And cart the sick from Lettermore :
A stinking load of rags and bones.

But you will go to Lettermore
When white sea-trout are on the run,
When purple glows between the rocks
About Lord Dudley's fishing box

Adown the road to Lettermore,
And wide seas tarnish in the sun.

And so you'll think of Lettermore
As a lost island of the blest :
With peasant lovers in a blue
Dim dusk, with heather drench'd in dew,
And the sweet peace of Lettermore
Remote and dreaming in the West.

Francis
Brett
Young

Francis
Brett
Young

SONG

Why have you stolen my delight
   In all the golden shows of Spring
When every cherry-tree is white
   And in the limes the thrushes sing,

O fickler than the April day,
   O brighter than the golden broom,
O blither than the thrushes' lay,
   O whiter than the cherry-bloom,

O sweeter than all things that blow . . .
   Why have you only left for me
The broom, the cherry's crown of snow,
   And thrushes in the linden-tree ?

THE LEANING ELM

Francis
Brett
Young

Before my window, in days of winter hoar
Huddled a mournful wood :
Smooth pillars of beech, domed chestnut, sycamore,
In stony sleep they stood :
But you, unhappy elm, the angry west
Had chosen from the rest,
Flung broken on your brothers' branches bare,
And left you leaning there
So dead that when the breath of winter cast
Wild snow upon the blast,
The other living branches, downward bowed,
Shook free their crystal shroud
And shed upon your blackened trunk beneath
Their livery of death. . . . .

On windless nights between the beechen bars
I watched cold stars
Throb whitely in the sky, and dreamily
Wondered if any life lay locked in thee :
If still the hidden sap secretly moved
As water in the icy winterbourne
Floweth unheard :
And half I pitied you your trance forlorn :
You could not hear, I thought, the voice of any bird,
The shadowy cries of bats in dim twilight
Or cool voices of owls crying by night . . .
Hunting by night under the hornéd moon :
Yet half I envied you your wintry swoon,
Till, on this morning mild, the sun, new-risen
Steals from his misty prison ;
The frozen fallows glow, the black trees shaken
In a clear flood of sunlight vibrating awaken :

Francis
Brett
Young And lo, your ravaged bole, beyond belief
Slenderly fledged anew with tender leaf
As pale as those twin vanes that break at last
In a tiny fan above the black beech-mast
Where no blade springeth green
But pallid bells of the shy helleborine.
What is this ecstasy that overwhelms
The dreaming earth ? See, the embrownéd elms
Crowding purple distances warm the depths of the
    wood :
A new-born wind tosses their tassels brown,
His white clouds dapple the down :
Into a green flame bursting the hedgerows stand.
Soon, with banners flying, Spring will walk the land . . .

There is no day for thee, my soul, like this,
No spring of lovely words. Nay, even the kiss
Of mortal love that maketh man divine
This light cannot outshine :
Nay, even poets, they whose frail hands catch
The shadow of vanishing beauty, may not match
This leafy ecstasy. Sweet words may cull
Such magical beauty as time may not destroy ;
But we, alas, are not more beautiful :
We cannot flower in beauty as in joy.
We sing, our muséd words are sped, and then
Poets are only men
Who age, and toil, and sicken. . . . This maim'd tree
May stand in leaf when I have ceased to be.

WILLIAM H. DAVIES

LOVELY DAMES

W. H.
Davies

Few are my books, but my small few have told
Of many a lovely dame that lived of old ;
And they have made me see those fatal charms
Of Helen, which brought Troy so many harms ;
And lovely Venus, when she stood so white
Close to her husband's forge in its red light.
I have seen Dian's beauty in my dreams,
When she had trained her looks in all the streams
She crossed to Latmos and Endymion ;
And Cleopatra's eyes, that hour they shone
The brighter for a pearl she drank to prove
How poor it was compared to her rich love :
But when I look on thee, love, thou dost give
Substance to those fine ghosts, and make them live.

W. H.
Davies

When yon full moon's with her white fleet of stars,
  And but one bird makes music in the grove ;
When you and I are breathing side by side,
  Where our two bodies make one shadow, love ;

Not for her beauty will I praise the moon,
  But that she lights thy purer face and throat ;
The only praise I'll give the nightingale
  Is that she draws from thee a richer note.

For, blinded with thy beauty, I am filled,
  Like Saul of Tarsus, with a greater light ;
When he had heard that warning voice in Heaven,
  And lost his eyes to find a deeper sight.

Come, let us sit in that deep silence then,
  Launched on love's rapids, with our passions proud
That makes all music hollow—though the lark
  Raves in his windy heights above a cloud.

ON HEARING MRS. WOODHOUSE PLAY THE HARPSICHORD

W. H. Davies

We poets pride ourselves on what
  We feel, and not what we achieve ;
The world may call our children fools,
  Enough for us that we conceive.
A little wren that loves the grass
Can be as proud as any lark
  That tumbles in a cloudless sky,
Up near the sun, till he becomes
  The apple of that shining eye.

So, lady, I would never dare
  To hear your music ev'ry day ;
With those great bursts that send my nerves
  In waves to pound my heart away ;
And those small notes that run like mice
Bewitched by light ; else on those keys—
  My tombs of song—you should engrave :
' My music, stronger than his own,
  Has made this poet my dumb slave.'

W. H.
Davies

When our two souls have left this mortal clay
    And, seeking mine, you think that mine is lost—
Look for me first in that Elysian glade
    Where Lesbia is, for whom the birds sing most.

What happy hearts those feathered mortals have,
    That sing so sweet when they're wet through in
        spring !
For in that month of May when leaves are young,
    Birds dream of song, and in their sleep they sing.

And when the spring has gone and they are dumb,
    Is it not fine to watch them at their play :
Is it not fine to see a bird that tries
    To stand upon the end of every spray ?

See how they tilt their pretty heads aside :
    When women make that move they always please.
What cosy homes birds make in leafy walls
    That Nature's love has ruined—and the trees.

Oft have I seen in fields the little birds
    Go in between a bullock's legs to eat ;
But what gives me most joy is when I see
    Snow on my doorstep, printed by their feet.

OH, SWEET CONTENT!

W. H.
Davies

Oh, sweet content, that turns the labourer's sweat
  To tears of joy, and shines the roughest face;
How often have I sought you high and low,
  And found you still in some lone quiet place;

Here, in my room, when full of happy dreams,
  With no life heard beyond that merry sound
Of moths that on my lighted ceiling kiss
  Their shadows as they dance and dance around;

Or in a garden, on a summer's night,
  When I have seen the dark and solemn air
Blink with the blind bats' wings, and heaven's bright
    face
  Twitch with the stars that shine in thousands there.

W. H.
Davies

When I sailed out of Baltimore
  With twice a thousand head of sheep,
They would not eat, they would not drink,
  But bleated o'er the deep.

Inside the pens we crawled each day,
  To sort the living from the dead ;
And when we reached the Mersey's mouth
  Had lost five hundred head.

Yet every night and day one sheep,
  That had no fear of man or sea,
Stuck through the bars its pleading face,
  And it was stroked by me.

And to the sheep-men standing near,
  ' You see,' I said, ' this one tame sheep :
It seems a child has lost her pet,
  And cried herself to sleep.'

So every time we passed it by,
  Sailing to England's slaughter-house,
Eight ragged sheep-men—tramps and thieves—
  Would stroke that sheep's black nose.

ENGLAND

W. H.
Davies

We have no grass locked up in ice so fast
That cattle cut their faces and at last,
When it is reached, must lie them down and starve,
With bleeding mouths that freeze too hard to move.
We have not that delirious state of cold
That makes men warm and sing when in Death's hold.
We have no roaring floods whose angry shocks
Can kill the fishes dashed against their rocks.
We have no winds that cut down street by street,
As easy as our scythes can cut down wheat.
No mountains here to spew their burning hearts
Into the valleys, on our human parts.
No earthquakes here, that ring church bells afar,
A hundred miles from where those earthquakes are.
We have no cause to set our dreaming eyes,
Like Arabs, on fresh streams in Paradise.
We have no wilds to harbour men that tell
More murders than they can remember well.
No woman here shall wake from her night's rest,
To find a snake is sucking at her breast.
Though I have travelled many and many a mile,
And had a man to clean my boots and smile
With teeth that had less bone in them than gold—
Give me this England now for all my world.

W. H.
Davies

THE BELL

It is the bell of death I hear,
Which tells me my own time is near,
When I must join those quiet souls
Where nothing lives but worms and moles ;
And not come through the grass again,
Like worms and moles, for breath or rain ;
Yet let none weep when my life's through,
For I myself have wept for few.

The only things that knew me well
Were children, dogs, and girls that fell ;
I bought poor children cakes and sweets,
Dogs heard my voice and danced the streets ;
And, gentle to a fallen lass,
I made her weep for what she was.
Good men and women know not me,
Nor love nor hate the mystery.

WALTER DE LA MARE

THE SUNKEN GARDEN

Walter De
La Mare

Speak not—whisper not ;
Here bloweth thyme and bergamot ;
Softly on the evening hour,
Secret herbs their spices shower,
Dark-spiked rosemary and myrrh,
Lean-stalked, purple lavender ;
Hides within her bosom, too,
All her sorrows, bitter rue.

Breathe not—trespass not ;
Of this green and darkling spot,
Latticed from the moon's beams,
Perchance a distant dreamer dreams ;
Perchance upon its darkening air,
The unseen ghosts of children fare,
Faintly swinging, sway and sweep,
Like lovely sea-flowers in its deep ;
While, unmoved, to watch and ward,
'Mid its gloomed and daisied sward,
Stands with bowed and dewy head
That one little leaden Lad.

Walter De
La Mare

MOONLIGHT

The far moon maketh lovers wise
. In her pale beauty trembling down,
Lending curved cheeks, dark lips, dark eyes,
A strangeness not their own.
And, though they shut their lids to kiss,
In starless darkness peace to win,
Even on that secret world from this
Her twilight enters in.

THE TRYST

Walter De
La Mare

Flee into some forgotten night and be
Of all dark long my moon-bright company :
Beyond the rumour even of Paradise come,
There, out of all remembrance, make our home :
Seek we some close hid shadow for our lair,
Hollowed by Noah's mouse beneath the chair
Wherein the Omnipotent, in slumber bound,
Nods till the piteous Trump of Judgment sound.
Perchance Leviathan of the deep sea
Would lease a lost mermaiden's grot to me,
There of your beauty we would joyance make—
A music wistful for the sea-nymph's sake :
Haply Elijah, o'er his spokes of fire,
Cresting steep Leo, or the heavenly Lyre,
Spied, tranced in azure of inanest space,
Some eyrie hostel, meet for human grace,
Where two might happy be—just you and I—
Lost in the uttermost of Eternity.
Think ! in Time's smallest clock's minutest beat
Might there not rest be found for wandering feet ?
Or, 'twixt the sleep and wake of Helen's dream,
Silence wherein to sing love's requiem ?

No, no. Nor earth, nor air, nor fire, nor deep
Could lull poor mortal longingness asleep.
Somewhere there nothing is ; and there lost Man
Shall win what changeless vague of peace he can.

Walter De
La Mare

THE LINNET

Upon this leafy bush
With thorns and roses in it,
Flutters a thing of light,
A twittering linnet.
And all the throbbing world
Of dew and sun and air
By this small parcel of life
Is made more fair ;
As if each bramble-spray
And mounded gold-wreathed furze,
Harebell and little thyme,
Were only hers ;
As if this beauty and grace
Did to one bird belong,
And, at a flutter of wing,
Might vanish in song.

THE VEIL

Walter De
La Mare

I think and think : yet still I fail—
Why must this lady wear a veil ?
Why thus elect to mask her face
Beneath that dainty web of lace ?
The tip of a small nose I see,
And two red lips, set curiously
Like twin-born berries on one stem,
And yet, she has netted even them.
Her eyes, 'tis plain, survey with ease
Whate'er to glance upon they please.
Yet, whether hazel, gray, or blue,
Or that even lovelier lilac hue,
I cannot guess : why—why deny
Such beauty to the passer-by ?
Out of a bush a nightingale
May expound his song ; from 'neath that veil
A happy mouth no doubt can make
English sound sweeter for its sake.
But then, why muffle in like this
What every blossomy wind would kiss ?
Why in that little night disguise
A daybreak face, those starry eyes ?

Walter De
La Mare

THE THREE STRANGERS

Far are those tranquil hills,
Dyed with fair evening's rose ;
On urgent, secret errand bent,
    A traveller goes.

Approach him strangers three,
Barefooted, cowled ; their eyes
Scan the lone, hastening solitary
    With dumb surmise.

One instant in close speech
With them he doth confer :
God-sped, he hasteneth on,
    That anxious traveller . . .

I was that man—in a dream :
And each world's night in vain
I patient wait on sleep to unveil
    Those vivid hills again.

Would that they three could know
How yet burns on in me
Love—from one lost in Paradise—
    For their grave courtesy.

THE OLD MEN

Walter De
La Mare

Old and alone, sit we,
Caged, riddle-rid men ;
Lost to earth's ' Listen ! ' and ' See ! '
Thought's ' Wherefore ? ' and ' When ? '

Only far memories stray
Of a past once lovely, but now
Wasted and faded away,
Like green leaves from the bough.

Vast broods the silence of night,
The ruinous moon
Lifts on our faces her light,
Whence all dreaming is gone.

We speak not ; trembles each head ;
In their sockets our eyes are still ;
Desire as cold as the dead ;
Without wonder or will.

And One, with a lanthorn, draws near,
At clash with the moon in our eyes :
' Where art thou ? ' he asks : ' I am here,'
One by one we arise.

And none lifts a hand to withhold
A friend from the touch of that foe :
Heart cries unto heart, ' Thou art old ! '
Yet reluctant, we go.

FARE WELL

When I lie where shades of darkness
Shall no more assail mine eyes,
Nor the rain make lamentation
    When the wind sighs ;
How will fare the world whose wonder
Was the very proof of me ?
Memory fades, must the remembered
    Perishing be ?

Oh, when this my dust surrenders
Hand, foot, lip, to dust again,
May those loved and loving faces
    Please other men !
May the rusting harvest hedgerow
Still the Traveller's Joy entwine,
And as happy children gather
    Posies once mine.

Look thy last on all things lovely,
Every hour. Let no night
Seal thy sense in deathly slumber
    Till to delight
Thou have paid thy utmost blessing ;
Since that all things thou wouldst praise
Beauty took from those who loved them
    In other days.

JOHN DRINKWATER

DEER

John
Drinkwater

Shy in their herding dwell the fallow deer.
They are spirits of wild sense. Nobody near
Comes upon their pastures. There a life they live,
Of sufficient beauty, phantom, fugitive
Treading as in jungles free leopards do,
Printless as evelight, instant as dew.
The great kine are patient, and home-coming sheep
Know our bidding. The fallow deer keep
Delicate and far their counsels wild,
Never to be folded reconciled
To the spoiling hand as the poor flocks are ;
Lightfoot, and swift, and unfamiliar,
These you may not hinder, unconfined
Beautiful flocks of the mind.

John
Drinkwater

MOONLIT APPLES

At the top of the house the apples are laid in rows,
And the skylight lets the moonlight in, and those
Apples are deep-sea apples of green. There goes
   A cloud on the moon in the autumn night.

A mouse in the wainscot scratches, and scratches, and
    then
There is no sound at the top of the house of men
Or mice ; and the cloud is blown, and the moon again
   Dapples the apples with deep-sea light.

They are lying in rows there, under the gloomy beams ;
On the sagging floor ; they gather the silver streams
Out of the moon, those moonlit apples of dreams,
   And quiet is the steep stair under.

In the corridors under there is nothing but sleep.
And stiller than ever on orchard boughs they keep
Tryst with the moon, and deep is the silence, deep
   On moon-washed apples of wonder.

SOUTHAMPTON BELLS

John
Drinkwater

I

Long ago some builder thrust
Heavenward in Southampton town
His spire and beamed his bells,
Largely conceiving from the dust
That pinnacle for ringing down
Orisons and Noëls.

In his imagination rang,
Through generations challenging
His peal on simple men,
Who, as the heart within him sang,
In daily townfaring should sing
By year and year again.

II

Now often to their ringing go
The bellmen with lean Time at heel,
Intent on daily cares ;
The bells ring high, the bells ring low,
The ringers ring the builder's peal
Of tidings unawares.

And all the bells might well be dumb
For any quickening in the street
Of customary ears ;
And so at last proud builders come
With dreams and virtues to defeat
Among the clouding years.

John
Drinkwater

Now, waiting on Southampton sea
For exile, through the silver night
I hear Noël ! Noël !
Through generations down to me
Your challenge, builder, comes aright,
Bell by obedient bell.

You wake an hour with me ; then wide
Though be the lapses of your sleep
You yet shall wake again ;
And thus, old builder, on the tide
Of immortality you keep
Your way from brain to brain.

CHORUS FROM *LINCOLN*

John
Drinkwater

You who have gone gathering
  Cornflowers and meadowsweet,
Heard the hazels glancing down
  On September eves,
Seen the homeward rooks on wing
  Over fields of golden wheat,
And the silver cups that crown
  Water-lily leaves ;

You who know the tenderness
  Of old men at eve-tide,
Coming from the hedgerows,
  Coming from the plough,
And the wandering caress
  Of winds upon the woodside,
When the crying yaffle goes
  Underneath the bough ;

You who mark the flowing
  Of sap upon the May-time,
And the waters welling
  From the watershed,
You who count the growing
  Of harvest and hay-time,
Knowing these the telling
  Of your daily bread ;

You who cherish courtesy
  With your fellows at your gate,
And about your hearthstone sit
  Under love's decrees,

John
Drinkwater

You who know that death will be
    Speaking with you soon or late,
Kinsmen, what is mother-wit
    But the light of these ?

Knowing these, what is there more
    For learning in your little years ?
Are not these all gospels bright
    Shining on your day ?
How then shall your hearts be sore
    With envy and her brood of fears,
How forget the words of light
    From the mountain-way . . .

Blessed are the merciful . . .
    Does not every threshold seek
Meadows and the flight of birds
    For compassion still ?
Blessed are the merciful . . .
    Are we pilgrims yet to speak
Out of Olivet the words
    Of knowledge and good-will ?

HABITATION

John
Drinkwater

High up in the sky there, now, you know,
In this May twilight, our cottage is asleep,
Tenantless, and no creature there to go
Near it but Mrs. Fry's fat cows, and sheep
Dove-coloured, as is Cotswold. No one hears
Under that cherry-tree the night-jars yet,
The windows are uncurtained ; on the stairs
Silence is but by tip-toe silence met.
All doors are fast there. It is a dwelling put by
From use for a little, or long, up there in the sky.

Empty ; a walled-in silence, in this twilight of May—
A home for lovers, and friendly withdrawing, and sleep,
With none to love there, nor laugh, nor climb from the day
To the candles and linen . . . Yet in the silence creep,
This minute, I know, little ghosts, little virtuous lives,
Breathing upon that still, insensible place,
Touching the latches, sorting the napkins and knives,
And such for the comfort of being, and bowls for the grace,
That roses will brim ; they are creeping from that room
    to this,
One room, and two, till the four are visited . . . they,
Little ghosts, little lives, are our thoughts in this twi-
    light of May,
Signs that even the curious man would miss,
Of travelling lovers to Cotswold, signs of an hour,
Very soon, when up from the valley in June will ride
Lovers by Lynch to Oakridge up in the wide
Bow of the hill, to a garden of lavender flower . . .
The doors are locked ; no foot falls ; the hearths are
    dumb—
But we are there—we are waiting ourselves who come.

John
Drinkwater

PASSAGE

When you deliberate the page
Of Alexander's pilgrimage,
Or say—' It is three years, or ten,
Since Easter slew Connolly's men,'
Or prudently to judgment come
Of Antony or Absalom,
And think how duly are designed
Case and instruction for the mind,
Remember then that also we,
In a moon's course, are history.

JOHN FREEMAN

O MUSE DIVINE

John
Freeman

O thou, my Muse,
Beside the Kentish River running
Through water-meads where dews
Tossed flashing at thy feet
And tossing flashed again
When the timid herd
By thy swift passing stirred
Up-leapt and ran ;

Thou that didst fleet
Thy shadow over dark October hills
By Aston, Weston, Saintbury, Willersey,
Winchcombe, and all the combes and hills
Of the green lonely land ;

Thou that in May
Once when I saw thee sunning
Thyself so lovely there
Than the flushed flower more fair
Fallen from the wild apple spray,
Didst rise and sprinkling sunlight with thy hand
Shadow-like disappear in the deep-shadowy hedges
Between forsaken Buckle Street and the sparse sedges
Of young twin-breasted Honeybourne ;—

O thou, my Muse,
Scarce longer seen than the brief hues
Of winter cloud that flames
Over the tarnished silver Thames ;
So often nearing,
As often disappearing,
With thy body's shadow brushing

John
Freeman

My brain at midnight, lightly touching ;
O yield thee, Muse, to me,
No more in dream delights and morn forgettings,
But in a ferny hollow I know well
And thou know'st well, warm-proof'd 'gainst the wind's
     frettings.
. . . Bring thou thyself, and there
In that warm ferny hollow where the sun
Slants one gold beam and no light else but thine
And my eyes' happy shine—
There, O lovely Muse,
Shall on thy shining body be begot,
Fruit of delights a many mingling in one,
Thy child and mine, a lovely shape and thought ;
My child and thine,
O Muse divine !

THE WAKERS

John
Freeman

The joyous morning ran and kissed the grass
And drew his fingers through her sleeping hair,
  And cried, ' Before thy flowers are well awake
  Rise, and the lingering darkness from thee shake.

' Before the daisy and the sorrel buy
Their brightness back from that close-folding night,
  Come, and the shadows from thy bosom shake,
  Awake from thy thick sleep, awake, awake ! '

Then the grass of that mounded meadow stirred
Above the Roman bones that may not stir
  Though joyous morning whispered, shouted, sang :
  The grass stirred as that happy music rang.

O, what a wondrous rustling everywhere !
The steady shadows shook and thinned and died,
  The shining grass flashed brightness back for bright-
     ness,
  And sleep was gone, and there was heavenly lightness.

As if she had found wings, light as the wind,
The grass flew, bent with the wind, from east to west,
  Chased by one wild grey cloud, and flashing all
  Her dews for happiness to hear morning call. . . .

But even as I stepped out the brightness dimmed,
I saw the fading edge of all delight.
  The sober morning waked the drowsy herds,
  And there was the old scolding of the birds.

THE BODY

When I had dreamed and dreamed what woman's beauty
    was,
    And how that beauty seen from unseen surely flowed,
I turned and dreamed again, but sleeping saw no more :
    My eyes shut and my mind with inward vision glowed.

' I did not think ! ' I cried, seeing that wavering shape
    That steadied and then wavered, as a cherry bough
        in June
Lifts and falls in the wind—each fruit a fruit of light ;
    And then she stood as clear as an unclouded moon.

As clear and still she stood, moonlike remotely near ;
    I saw and heard her breathe, I years and years away.
Her light streamed through the years, I saw her clear
        and still,
    Shape and spirit together mingling night with day.

Water falling, falling with the curve of time
    Over green-hued rock, then plunging to its pool
Far, far below, a falling spear of light ;
    Water falling golden from the sun but moonlike cool :

Water has the curve of her shoulder and breast,
    Water falls as straight as her body rose,
Water her brightness has from neck to still feet,
    Water crystal-cold as her cold body flows.

But not water has the colour I saw when I dreamed,
    Nor water such strength has. I joyed to behold
How the blood lit her body with lamps of fire
    And made the flesh glow that like water gleamed cold,

A flame in her arms and in each finger flame,
    And flame in her bosom, flame above, below,
The curve of climbing flame in her waist and her thighs;
    From foot to head did flame into red flame flow.

John Freeman

I knew how beauty seen from unseen must rise,
    How the body's joy for more than body's use was
      made.
I knew then how the body is the body of the mind,
    And how the mind's own fire beneath the cool skin
      played.

O shape that once to have seen is to see evermore,
    Falling stream that falls to the deeps of the mind,
Fire that once lit burns while aught burns in the world,
    Foot to head a flame moving in the spirit's wind !

If these eyes could see what these eyes have not seen—
    The inward vision clear—how should I look, for joy,
Knowing that beauty's self rose visible in the world
    Over age that darkens, and griefs that destroy ?

John
Freeman

TEN O'CLOCK NO MORE*

The wind has thrown
The boldest of trees down.
Now disgraced it lies,
Naked in spring beneath the drifting skies,
Naked and still.

It was the wind
So furious and blind
That scourged half England through,
Ruining the fairest where most fair it grew
By dell and hill,

And springing here,
The black clouds dragging near,
Against this lonely elm
Thrust all his strength to maim and overwhelm
In one wild shock.

As in the deep
Satisfaction of dark sleep
The tree her dream dreamed on,
And woke to feel the wind's arms round her thrown
And her head rock.

And the wind raught
Her ageing boughs and caught
Her body fast again.
Then in one agony of age, grief, pain,
She fell and died.

* *Ten o'clock* is the name of a tall tree that crowned the eastern Cotswolds.

64

Her noble height,
Branches that loved the light,
Her music and cool shade,
Her memories and all of her is dead
On the hill side.

But the wind stooped,
With madness tired, and drooped
In the soft valley and slept,
While morning strangely round the hush'd tree crept
And called in vain.

The birds fed where
The roots uptorn and bare
Thrust shameful at the sky ;
And pewits round the tree would dip and cry
With the old pain.

' Ten o'clock's gone ! '
Said sadly every one.
And mothers looking thought
Of sons and husbands far away that fought :—
And looked again.

John
Freeman

THE FUGITIVE

In the hush of early even
The clouds came flocking over,
Till the last wind fell from heaven
    And no bird cried.

Darkly the clouds were flocking,
Shadows moved and deepened,
Then paused ; the poplar's rocking
    Ceased ; the light hung still

Like a painted thing, and deadly.
Then from the cloud's side flickered
Sharp lightning, thrusting madly
    At the cowering fields.

Thrice the fierce cloud lighten'd,
Down the hill slow thunder trembled ;
Day in her cave grew frightened,
    Crept away, and died.

THE ALDE

John
Freeman

How near I walked to Love,
How long, I cannot tell.
I was like the Alde that flows
Quietly through green level lands,
So quietly, it knows
Their shape, their greenness and their shadows well ;
And then undreamingly for miles it goes
And silently, beside the sea.

Seamews circle over,
The winter wildfowl wings,
Long and green the grasses wave
Between the river and the sea.
The sea's cry, wild or grave,
From bank to low bank of the river rings ;
But the uncertain river though it crave
The sea, knows not the sea.

Was that indeed salt wind ?
Came that noise from falling
Wild waters on a stony shore ?
Oh, what is this new troubling tide
Of eager waves that pour
Around and over, leaping, parting, recalling ? . . .
How near I moved (as day to same day wore)
And silently, beside the sea !

John
Freeman

Thy hand my hand,
Thine eyes my eyes,
All of thee
Caught and confused with me :
My hand thy hand,
My eyes thine eyes,
All of me
Sunken and discovered anew in thee. . . .

No : still
A foreign mind,
A thought
By other yet uncaught ;
A secret will
Strange as the wind :
The heart of thee
Bewildering with strange fire the heart in me.

Hand touches hand,
Eye to eye beckons,
But who shall guess
Another's loneliness ?
Though hand grasp hand,
Though the eye quickens,
Still lone as night
Remain thy spirit and mine, past touch and sight.

NIGHT AND NIGHT

John
Freeman

The earth is purple in the evening light,
The grass is graver green.
The gold among the meadows darker glows,
In the quieted air the blackbird sings more loud.
The sky has lost its rose—
Nothing more than this candle now shines bright.

Were there but natural night, how easy were
The putting-by of sense
At the day's end, and if no heavier air
Came o'er the mind in a thick-falling cloud.
But now there is no light
Within ; and to this innocent night how dark my
night !

The roaming sheep, forbidden to roam far,
Were stayed within the shadow of his eye.
The sheep-dog on that unseen shadow's edge
Moved, halted, barked, while the tall shepherd stood
Unmoving, leaned upon a sarsen stone,
Looking at the rain that curtained the bare hills
And drew the smoking curtain near and near !—
Tawny, bush-faced, with cloak and staff, and flask
And bright brass-ribb'd umbrella, standing stone
Against the veinless, senseless sarsen stone.
The Roman Road hard by, the green Ridge Way,
Not older seemed, nor calmer the long barrows
Of bones and memories of ancient days
Than the tall shepherd with his craft of days
Older than Roman or the oldest caveman,
When, in the generation of all living,
Sheep and kine flocked in the Aryan valley and
The first herd with his voice and skill of water
Fleetest of foot, led them into green pastures,
From perished pastures to new green. I saw
The herdsmen everywhere about the world,
And herdsmen of all time, fierce, lonely, wise,
Herds of Arabia and Syria
And Thessaly, and longer-winter'd climes ;
And this lone herd, ages before England was,
Pelt-clad, and armed with flint-tipped ashen sap,
Watching his flocks, and those far flocks of stars
Slow moving as the heavenly shepherd willed
And at dawn shut into the sunny fold.

WILFRID WILSON GIBSON

WINGS

Wilfrid
Wilson
Gibson

As a blue-necked mallard alighting in a pool
Among marsh-marigolds and splashing wet
Green leaves and yellow blooms, like jewels set
In bright, black mud, with clear drops crystal-cool,
Bringing keen savours of the sea and stir
Of windy spaces where wild sunsets flame
To that dark inland dyke, the thought of her
Into my brooding stagnant being came.

And all my senses quickened into life,
Tingling and glittering, and the salt and fire
Sang through my singing blood in eager strife
Until through crystal airs we seemed to be
Soaring together, one fleet-winged desire
Of windy sunsets and the wandering sea.

Wilfrid
Wilson
Gibson

Somewhere, somewhen I've seen,
But where or when I'll never know,
Parrots of shrilly green
With crests of shriller scarlet flying
Out of black cedars as the sun was dying
Against cold peaks of snow.

From what forgotten life
Of other worlds I cannot tell
Flashes that screeching strife ;
Yet the shrill colour and shrill crying
Sing through my blood and set my heart replying
And jangling like a bell.

THE CAKEWALK

Wilfrid
Wilson
Gibson

In smoky lamplight of a Smyrna Café,
He saw them, seven solemn negroes dancing,
With faces rapt and out-thrust bellies prancing
In a slow solemn ceremonial cakewalk,
Dancing and prancing to the sombre tom-tom
Thumped by a crookbacked grizzled negro squatting.
And as he watched . . . within the steamy twilight
Of swampy forest in rank greenness rotting,
That sombre tom-tom at his heartstrings strumming
Set all his sinews twitching, and a singing
Of cold fire through his blood—and he was dancing
Among his fellows in the dank green twilight
With naked, oiled, bronze-gleaming bodies swinging
In a rapt holy everlasting cakewalk
For evermore in slow procession prancing.

Wilfrid
Wilson
Gibson

DRIFTWOOD

Black spars of driftwood burn to peacock flames,
Sea-emeralds and sea-purples and sea-blues,
And all the innumerable ever-changing hues
That haunt the changeless deeps but have no names,
Flicker and spire in our enchanted sight :
And as we gaze, the unsearchable mystery,
The unfathomed cold salt magic of the sea,
Shines clear before us in the quiet night.

We know the secret that Ulysses sought,
That moonstruck mariners since time began
Snatched at a drowning hazard—strangely brought
To our homekeeping hearts in drifting spars
We chanced to kindle under the cold stars—
The secret in the ocean-heart of man.

QUIET

Wilfrid
Wilson
Gibson

Only the footprints of the partridge run
Over the billowy drifts on the mountain-side ;
And now on level wings the brown birds glide
Following the snowy curves, and in the sun
Bright birds of gold above the stainless white
They move, and as the pale blue shadows move,
With them my heart glides on in golden flight
Over the hills of quiet to my love.

Storm-shaken, racked with terror through the long
Tempestuous night, in the quiet blue of morn
Love drinks the crystal airs, and peace newborn
Within his troubled heart, on wings aglow
Soars into rapture, as from the quiet snow
The golden birds ; and out of silence, song.

Wilfrid
Wilson
Gibson

REVEILLE

Still bathed in its moonlight slumber, the little white
house by the cedar
Stands silent against the red dawn ;
And nothing I know of who sleeps there, to the travail
of day yet unwakened,
Behind the blue curtains undrawn :

But I dream as we march down the roadway, ringing
loud and white-rimed in the moonlight,
Of a little dark house on a hill
Wherein when the battle is over, to the rapture of day
yet unwakened,
We shall slumber as dreamless and still.

ROBERT GRAVES

A BALLAD OF NURSERY RHYME

Robert
Graves

Strawberries that in gardens grow
   Are plump and juicy fine,
But sweeter far as wise men know
   Spring from the woodland vine.

No need for bowl or silver spoon,
   Sugar or spice or cream,
Has the wild berry plucked in June
   Beside the trickling stream.

One such to melt at the tongue's root,
   Confounding taste with scent,
Beats a full peck of garden fruit :
   Which points my argument.

May sudden justice overtake
   And snap the froward pen,
That old and palsied poets shake
   Against the minds of men ;

Blasphemers trusting to hold caught
   In far-flung webs of ink
The utmost ends of human thought,
   Till nothing's left to think.

But may the gift of heavenly peace
   And glory for all time
Keep the boy Tom who tending geese
   First made the nursery rhyme.

By the brookside one August day,
   Using the sun for clock,
Tom whiled the languid hours away
   Beside his scattering flock,

Robert
Graves

Carving with a sharp pointed stone
  On a broad slab of slate
The famous lives of Jumping Joan,
  Dan Fox and Greedy Kate ;

Rhyming of wolves and bears and birds,
  Spain, Scotland, Babylon,
That sister Kate might learn the words
  To tell to Toddling John.

But Kate, who could not stay content
  To learn her lesson pat,
New beauty to the rough lines lent
  By changing this or that ;

And she herself set fresh things down
  In corners of her slate,
Of lambs and lanes and London Town.
  God's blessing fall on Kate !

The baby loved the simple sound,
  With jolly glee he shook,
And soon the lines grew smooth and round
  Like pebbles in Tom's brook,

From mouth to mouth told and retold
  By children sprawled at ease
Before the fire in winter's cold,
  In June beneath tall trees ;

Till though long lost are stone and slate,
  Though the brook no more runs,
And dead long time are Tom, John, Kate,
  Their sons and their sons' sons ;

Yet, as when Time with stealthy tread
   Lays the rich garden waste,
The woodland berry ripe and red
   Fails not in scent or taste,

So these same rhymes shall still be told
   To children yet unborn,
While false philosophy growing old
   Fades and is killed by scorn.

Robert
Graves

Robert
Graves

A FROSTY NIGHT

Mother :   Alice, dear, what ails you,
             Dazed and white and shaken ?
             Has the chill night numbed you ?
             Is it fright you have taken ?

Alice :   Mother I am very well,
             I felt never better ;
             Mother, do not hold me so,
             Let me write my letter.

Mother :   Sweet, my dear, what ails you ?
Alice :   No, but I am well.
             The night was cold and frosty,
             There's no more to tell.

Mother :   Ay, the night was frosty,
             Coldly gaped the moon,
             Yet the birds seemed twittering
             Through green boughs of June.

             Soft and thick the snow lay,
             Stars danced in the sky.
             Not all the lambs of May-day
             Skip so bold and high.

             Your feet were dancing, Alice,
             Seemed to dance on air,
             You looked a ghost or angel
             In the starlight there.

             Your eyes were frosted starlight,
             Your heart, fire, and snow.
             Who was it said ' I love you ? '
Alice :   Mother, let me go !

TRUE JOHNNY

Robert
Graves

Mary :   Johnny, sweetheart, can you be true
To all those famous vows you've made ?
Will you love me as I love you
Until we both in earth are laid ?
Or shall the old wives nod and say
' His love was only for a day,
        The mood goes by,
        His fancies fly,
And Mary's left to sigh.'

Johnny :   Mary, alas, you've hit the truth,
And I with grief can but admit
Hot-blooded haste controls my youth,
My idle fancies veer and flit
From flower to flower, from tree to tree,
And when the moment catches me
        Oh, love goes by,
        Away I fly,
And leave my girl to sigh.

Mary :   Could you but now foretell the day,
Johnny, when this sad thing must be,
When light and gay you'll turn away
And laugh and break the heart in me ?
For like a nut for true love's sake
My empty heart shall crack and break,
        When fancies fly
        And love goes by
And Mary's left to die.

Johnny :   When the sun turns against the clock,
When Avon waters upward flow,

Robert
Graves

When eggs are laid by barn-door cock,
When dusty hens do strut and crow,
When up is down, when left is right,
Oh, then I'll break the troth I plight,
    With careless eye
    Away I'll fly
And Mary here shall die

THE CUPBOARD

Robert
Graves

Mother :   What's in that cupboard, Mary ?
Mary :   Which cupboard, mother dear ?
Mother :   The cupboard of red mahogany
        With handles shining clear.

Mary :   That cupboard, dearest mother,
        With shining crystal handles ?
    There's nought inside but rags and jags
        And yellow tallow candles.

Mother :   What's in that cupboard, Mary ?
Mary :   Which cupboard, mother mine ?
Mother :   That cupboard stands in your sunny chamber,
        The silver corners shine.

Mary :   There's nothing there inside, mother,
        But wool and thread and flax,
    And bits of faded silk and velvet
        And candles of white wax.

Mother :   What's in that cupboard, Mary ?
        And this time tell me true.
Mary :   White clothes for an unborn baby, mother . .
        But what's the truth to you ?

Robert
Graves

THE VOICE OF BEAUTY DROWNED

Cry from the thicket my heart's bird !
The other birds woke all around ;
Rising with toot and howl they stirred
Their plumage, broke the trembling sound,
They craned their necks, they fluttered wings,
' While we are silent no one sings,
And while we sing you hush your throat,
Or tune your melody to our note.'

Cry from the thicket my heart's bird !
The screams and hootings rose again :
They gaped with raucous beaks, they whirred
Their noisy plumage ; small but plain
The lonely hidden singer made
A well of grief within the glade.
' Whist, silly fool, be off,' they shout,
' Or we'll come pluck your feathers out.'

Cry from the thicket my heart's bird !
Slight and small the lovely cry
Came trickling down, but no one heard ;
Parrot and cuckoo, crow, magpie,
Jarred horrid notes, the jangling jay
Ripped the fine threads of song away ;
For why should peeping chick aspire
To challenge their loud woodland choir ?

Cried it so sweet, that unseen bird ?
Lovelier could no music be,
Clearer than water, soft as curd,
Fresh as the blossomed cherry tree.

How sang the others all around ?　　　　　　Robert
Piercing and harsh, a maddening sound,　　　Graves
With *Pretty Poll*, *Tuwit-tuwoo*
Peewit, *Caw Caw*, *Cuckoo-Cuckoo*.

How went the song, how looked the bird ?
If I could tell, if I could show
With one quick phrase, one lightning word,
I'd learn you more than poets know ;
For poets, could they only catch
Of that forgotten tune one snatch,
Would build it up in song or sonnet,
And found their whole life's fame upon it.

Robert
Graves

This is a wild land, country of my choice,
　　With harsh craggy mountain, moor ample and bare.
Seldom in these acres is heard any voice
　　But voice of cold water that runs here and there
　　Through rocks and lank heather growing without care.
No mice in the heath run nor no birds cry
For fear of the dark speck that floats in the sky.

He soars and he hovers rocking on his wings,
　　He scans his wide parish with a sharp eye,
He catches the trembling of small hidden things,
　　He tears them in pieces dropping from the sky :
　　Tenderness and pity the land will deny,
Where life is but nourished from water and rock,
A hardy adventure, full of fear and shock.

Time has never journeyed to this lost land,
　　Crakeberries and heather bloom out of date,
The rocks jut, the streams flow singing on either hand,
　　Careless if the season be early or late.
　　The skies wander overhead, now blue now slate :
Winter would be known by his cold cutting snow
If June did not borrow his armour also.

Yet this is my country beloved by me best,
　　The first land that rose from Chaos and the Flood,
Nursing no fat valleys for comfort and rest,
　　Trampled by no hard hooves, stained with no blood.
　　Bold immortal country whose hill-tops have stood
Strongholds for the proud gods when on earth they go,
Terror for fat burghers in far plains below.

D. H. LAWRENCE

SEVEN SEALS

D. H.
Lawrence

Since this is the last night I keep you home,
Come, I will consecrate you for the journey.

Rather I had you would not go. Nay come,
I will not again reproach you. Lie back
And let me love you a long time ere you go.
For you are sullen-hearted still, and lack
The will to love me. But even so
I will set a seal upon you from my lip,
Will set a guard of honour at each door,
Seal up each channel out of which might slip
Your love for me.

        I kiss your mouth. Ah, love,
Could I but seal its ruddy, shining spring
Of passion, parch it up, destroy, remove
Its softly-stirring, crimson welling-up
Of kisses ! Oh, help me, God ! Here at the source
I'd lie for ever drinking and drawing in
Your fountains, as heaven drinks from out their course
The floods.

        I close your ears with kisses
And seal your nostrils ; and round your neck you'll
    wear—
Nay, let me work—a delicate chain of kisses.
Like beads they go around, and not one misses
To touch its fellow on either side.

        And there
Full mid-between the champaign of your breast
I place a great and burning seal of love

D. H.
Lawrence
Like a dark rose, a mystery of rest
On the slow bubbling of your rhythmic heart.
Nay, I persist, and very faith shall keep
You integral to me. Each door, each mystic port
Of egress from you I will seal and steep
In perfect chrism.

                 Now it is done. The mort
Will sound in heaven before it is undone.

But let me finish what I have begun
And shirt you now invulnerable in the mail
Of iron kisses, kisses linked like steel.
Put greaves upon your thighs and knees, and frail
Webbing of steel on your feet. So you shall feel
Ensheathed invulnerable with me, with seven
Great seals upon your outgoings, and woven
Chain of my mystic will wrapped perfectly
Upon you, wrapped in indomitable me.

94

HAROLD MONRO

GRAVITY

Harold
Monro

I

Fit for perpetual worship is the power
That holds our bodies safely to the earth.

When people talk of their domestic gods,
Then privately I think of You.

We ride through space upon your shoulders
Conveniently and lightly set,
And, so accustomed, we relax our hold,
Forget the gentle motion of your body—
But You do not forget.

Sometimes you breathe a little faster,
Or move a muscle :
Then we remember you, O Master.

II

When people meet in reverent groups
And sing to their domestic God,
You, all the time, dear tyrant, (How I laugh !)
Could, without effort, place your hand among them,
And sprinkle them about the desert.

But all your ways are carefully ordered,
For you have never questioned duty.
We watch your everlasting combinations ;
We call them Fate ; we turn them to our pleasure,
And when they most delight us, call them beauty.

97

Harold
Monro

III

I rest my body on your grass,
And let my brain repose in you ;
I feel these living moments pass,
And, from within myself to those far places
To be imagined in your times and spaces,
Deliberate the various acts you do :—

Sorting and re-arranging worlds of Matter
Keenly and wisely. Thus you brought our earth
Through stages, and from purpose back to purpose,
From fire to fog, to dust, to birth
Through beast to man, who led himself to brain—
Then you invoked him back to dust again.

By leave of you he places stone on stone ;
He scatters seed : you are at once the prop
Among the long roots of his fragile crop.
You manufacture for him, and insure
House, harvest, implement and furniture,
And hold them all secure.

IV

The hill . . . The trees . . . From underneath
I feel You pull me with your hand :
Through my firm feet up to my heart
You hold me,—You are in the land,
Reposing underneath the hill.

You keep my balance and my growth.
I lift a foot, but where I go
You follow : you, the ever-strong,
Control the smallest thing I do.

I have some little human power   Harold
To turn your purpose to my end,   Monro
For which I thank you every hour.
I stand at worship, while you send
Thrills up my body to my heart,
And I am all in love to know
How by your strength you keep me part
Of earth, which cannot let me go ;
How everything I see around,
Whether it can or cannot move,
Is granted liberty of ground,
And freedom to enjoy your love ;

Though you are silent always, and, alone
To You yourself, your power remains unknown.

GOLDFISH

They are the angels of that watery world,
With so much knowledge that they just aspire
To move themselves on golden fins,
Or fill their paradise with fire
By darting suddenly from end to end.

Glowing a thousand centuries behind
In pools half-recollected of the mind,
Their large eyes stare and stare, but do not see
Beyond those curtains of Eternity.

When twilight flows into the room
And air becomes like water, you can feel
Their movements growing larger in the gloom,
And you are led
Backward to where they live beyond the dead.

But in the morning, when the seven rays
Of London sunlight one by one incline,
They glide to meet them, and their gulping lips
Suck the light in, so they are caught and played
Like salmon on a heavenly fishing line.

* * * *

Ghosts on a twilight floor,
Moving about behind their watery door,
Breathing and yet not breathing day and night,
They give the house some gleam of faint delight.

DOG

Harold
Monro

You little friend, your nose is ready ; you sniff,
Asking for that expected walk,
(Your nostrils full of the happy rabbit-whiff)
And almost talk.

And so the moment becomes a moving force ;
Coats glide down from their pegs in the humble dark ;
The sticks grow live to the stride of their vagrant course.
You scamper the stairs,
Your body informed with the scent and the track and
    the mark
Of stoats and weasels, moles and badgers and hares.

We are going *out*. You know the pitch of the word,
Probing the tone of thought as it comes through fog
And reaches by devious means (half-smelt, half-heard)
The four-legged brain of a walk-ecstatic dog.

Out in the garden your head is already low.
(Can you smell the rose ? Ah, no.)
But your limbs can draw
Life from the earth through the touch of your padded paw.

Now, sending a little look to us behind,
Who follow slowly the track of your lovely play,
You carry our bodies forward away from mind
Into the light and fun of your useless day.

       *   *   *   *

Thus, for your walk, we took ourselves, and went
Out by the hedge and the tree to the open ground.
You ran, in delightful strata of wafted scent,

Harold
Monro

Over the hill without seeing the view ;
Beauty is smell upon primitive smell to you :
To you, as to us, it is distant and rarely found.

Home . . . and further joy will be surely there :
Supper waiting full of the taste of bone.
You throw up your nose again, and sniff, and stare
For the rapture known
Of the quick wild gorge of food and the still lie-down
While your people talk above you in the light
Of candles, and your dreams will merge and drown
Into the bed-delicious hours of night.

THE NIGHTINGALE NEAR THE HOUSE   Harold
Monro

Here is the soundless cypress on the lawn :
It listens, listens. Taller trees beyond
Listen. The moon at the unruffled pond
    Stares. And you sing, you sing.

That star-enchanted song falls through the air
From lawn to lawn down terraces of sound,
Darts in white arrows on the shadowed ground ;
    And all the night you sing.

My dreams are flowers to which you are a bee
As all night long I listen, and my brain
Receives your song, then loses it again
    In moonlight on the lawn.

Now is your voice a marble high and white,
Then like a mist on fields of paradise,
Now is a raging fire, then is like ice,
    Then breaks, and it is dawn.

MAN CARRYING BALE

The tough hand closes gently on the load ;
   Out of the mind, a voice
Calls ' Lift ! ' and the arms, remembering well their
     work,
   Lengthen and pause for help.
Then a slow ripple flows from head to foot
While all the muscles call to one another :
   ' Lift ! ' and the bulging bale
   Floats like a butterfly in June.

So moved the earliest carrier of bales,
   And the same watchful sun
Glowed through his body feeding it with light.
   So will the last one move,
And halt, and dip his head, and lay his load
Down, and the muscles will relax and tremble.
   Earth, you designed your man
Beautiful both in labour and repose.

THOMAS MOULT

FOR BESSIE, SEATED BY ME IN THE GARDEN

Thomas Moult

To the heart, to the heart the white petals
Quietly fall.
Memory is a little wind, and magical
The dreaming hours.
As a breath they fall, as a sigh ;
Green garden hours too langorous to waken,
White leaves of blossomy tree wind-shaken :
As a breath, a sigh,
As the slow white drift
Of a butterfly.
Flower-wings falling, wings of branches
One after one at wind's droop dipping ;
Then with the lift
Of the air's soft breath, in sudden avalanches
Slipping.
Quietly, quietly the June wind flings
White wings,
White petals, past the footpath flowers
Down my dreaming hours.
At the heart, at the heart the butterfly settles.
As a breath, a sigh
all the petals of hours, of the white-leafed flowers,
all the petalled wings of the butterfly.
To my heart, to my heart the white petals
Quietly fall.

To the years, other years, old and wistful
Drifts my dream.
Petal-patined the dream, white-mistful
As the dew-sweet haunt of the dim whitebeam
Because of memory, a little wind . . .

Thomas Moult

It is the gossamer-float of the butterfly
This drift of dream
From the sweet of to-day to the sweet
Of days long drifted by.
It is the drift of the butterfly, it is the fleet
Drift of petals which my noon has thinned,
It is the ebbing out of my life, of the petals of days.
To the years, other years, drifts my dream. . . .
Through the haze
Of summers long ago
Love's entrancements flow,
A blue-green pageant of earth,
A green-blue pageant of sky,
As a stream,
Flooding back with lovely delta to my heart.
Lo the petalled leafage is finer, under the feet
The coarse soil with a rainbow's worth
Of delicate colours lies enamelled,
Translucently glowing, shining.
Each balmy breath of the hours
From eastern gleam to westward gloam
Is meaning-full as the falling flowers :
It is a crystal syllable
For love's defining,
It is love alone can spell——
Yea, Love remains : after this drift of days
Love is here, Love is not dumb.
The touch of a silken hand, comradely, untrammell
Is in the sunlight, a bright glance
On every ripple of yonder waterways,
A whisper in the dance
Of green shadows ;
Nor shall the sunlight be shut out even from th
    dark.

Beyond the garden heavy oaks are buoyant on
    the meadows,
Their rugged bark
No longer rough,
But chastened and refinèd in the glowing eyes of Love.
Around us the petals fulfil
Their measure and fall, precious the petals are still.
For Love they once were gathered, they are gathered
    for Love again,
Whose glance is on the water,
Whose whisper is in the green shadows.
In the same comrade-hand whose touch is in the sun-
    light,
They are lying again.
Here Love is . . . Love only of all things outstays
The drift of petals, the drift of days,
Petals of hours,
Of white-leafed flowers,
Petalled wings of the butterfly,
Drifting, quietly drifting by
As a breath, a sigh. . . .

Thomas
Moult

Brown earth, sun-soaked,
Beneath his head
And over the quiet limbs. . . .
Through time unreckonèd
Lay this brown earth for him. Now is he come.
Truly he hath a sweet bed.

The perfume shed
From invisible gardens is chaliced by kindly airs
And carried for welcome to the stranger.
Long seasons ere he came, this wilderness
They habited.

They, and the mist of stars
Down-spread
About him as a hush of vespering birds.
They, and the sun, the moon :
Naught now denies him the moon's coming,
Nor the morning trail of gold,
The luminous print of evening, red
At the sun's tread.

The brown earth holds him.
The stars and little winds, the friendly moon
And sun attend in turn his rest.
They linger above him, softly moving. They are gracious
And gently-wise : as though remembering how his
        hunger,
His kinship, knew them once but blindly
In thoughts unsaid,
As a dream that fled.

So is he theirs assuredly as the seasons.   Thomas
So is his sleep by them for ever companioned.   Moult
. . . And, perchance, by the voices of bright children
    playing
And knowing not : by the echo of young laughter
When their dancing is sped.

Truly he hath a sweet bed.

Thomas
Moult

This cool quiet of trees
In the grey dusk of the north,
In the green half-dusk of the west,
Where fires still glow ;
These glimmering fantasies
Of foliage branching forth
And drooping into rest ;
Ye lovers, know
That in your wanderings
Beneath this arching brake
Ye must attune your love
To hushéd words.
For here is the dreaming wisdom of
The unmovable things . . .
　　　And more :—walk softly, lest ye wake
A thousand sleeping birds.

ROBERT NICHOLS

Photo by Malcom Arbuthnot.

Mr. Robert Nichols.

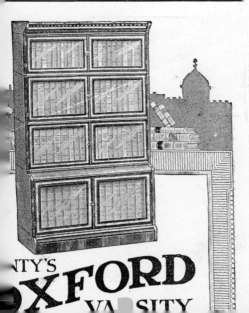

THE SPRIG OF LIME

Robert
Nichols

He lay, and those who watched him were amazed
To see unheralded beneath the lids
Twin tears, new-gathered at the price of pain,
Start and at once run crookedly athwart
Cheeks channelled long by pain, never by tears.
So desolate too the sigh next uttered
They had wept also, but his great lips moved,
And bending down one heard, ' *A sprig of lime ;*
Bring me a sprig of lime.' Whereat she stole
With dumb signs forth to pluck the thing he craved.

So lay he till a lime-twig had been snapped
From some still branch that swept the outer grass
Far from the silver pillar of the bole
Which mounting past the house's crusted roof
Split into massy limbs, crossed boughs, a maze
Of close-compacted intercontorted staffs
Bowered in foliage wherethrough the sun
Shot sudden showers of light or crystal spars
Or wavered in a green and vitreous flood.
And all the while in faint and fainter tones
Scarce audible on deepened evening's hush
He framed his curious and last request
For ' *lime, a sprig of lime.*' Her trembling hand
Closed his loose fingers on the awkward stem
Covered above with gentle heart-shaped leaves
And under dangling, pale as honey-wax,
Square clusters of sweet-scented starry flowers.

She laid his bent arm back upon his breast,
Then watched above white knuckles clenched in prayer.

Robert
Nichols

He never moved. Only at last his eyes
Opened, then brightened in such avid gaze
She feared the coma mastered him again . . .
But no ; strange sobs rose chuckling in his throat,
A stranger ecstasy suffused the flesh
Of that just mask so sun-dried, gouged and old
Which few—too few !—had loved, too many feared.
' Father ! ' she cried ; ' Father ! '
                 He did not hear.

She knelt and kneeling drank the scent of limes,
Blown round the slow blind by a vesperal gust,
Till the room swam. So the lime-incense blew
Into her life as once it had in his,
Though how and when and with what ageless charge
Of sorrow and deep joy how could she know ?

Sweet lime that often at the height of noon
Diffusing dizzy fragrance from your boughs,
Tasselled with blossoms more innumerable
Than the black bees, the uproar of whose toil
Filled your green vaults, winning such metheglyn
As clouds their sappy cells, distil, as once
Ye used, your sunniest emanations
Toward the window where a woman kneels—
She who within that room in childish hours
Lay through the lasting murmur of blanch'd noon
Behind the sultry blind, now full now flat,
Drinking anew of every odorous breath,
Supremely happy in her ignorance
Of Time that hastens hourly and of Death
Who need not haste. Scatter your fumes, O lime,
Loose from each hispid star of citron bloom,
Tangled beneath the labyrinthine boughs,

116

Cloud on such stinging cloud of exhalations
As reek of youth, fierce life and summer's prime,
Though hardly now shall he in that dusk room
Savour your sweetness, since the very sprig,
Profuse of blossom and of essences,
He smells not, who in a paltering hand
Clasps it laid close his peaked and gleaming face
Propped in the pillow. Breathe silent, lofty lime,
Your curfew secrets out in fervid scent
To the attendant shadows ! Tinge the air
Of the midsummer night that now begins,
At an owl's oaring flight from dusk to dusk
And downward caper of the giddy bat
Hawking against the lustre of bare skies,
With something of th' unfathomable bliss
He, who lies dying there, knew once of old
In the serene trance of a summer night
When with th' abundance of his young bride's hair
Loosed on his breast he lay and dared not sleep,
Listening for the scarce motion of your boughs,
Which sighed with bliss as she with blissful sleep,
And drinking desperately each honied wave
Of perfume wafted past the ghostly blind
Knew first th' implacable and bitter sense
Of Time that hastes and Death who need not haste.
Shed your last sweetness, limes !
                    But now no more.
She, fruit of that night's love, she heeds you not,
Who bent, compassionate, to the dim floor
Takes up the sprig of lime and presses it
In pain against the stumbling of her heart,
Knowing, untold, he cannot need it now.

Robert
Nichols

Robert
Nichols

SEVENTEEN

For Anne.

All the loud winds were in the garden wood,
All shadows joyfuller than lissom hounds
Doubled in chasing, all exultant clouds
That ever flung fierce mist and eddying fire
Across heavens deeper than blue polar seas
Fled over the sceptre-spikes of the chestnuts,
Over the speckle of the wych-elms' green.
She shouted ; then stood still, hushed and abashed
To hear her voice so shrill in that gay roar,
And suddenly her eyelashes were dimmed,
Caught in tense tears of spiritual joy ;
For there were daffodils which sprightly shook
Ten thousand ruffling heads throughout the wood,
And every flower of those delighting flowers
Laughed, nodding to her, till she clapped her hands
Crying ' O daffies, could you only speak ! '

But there was more. A jay with skyblue shaft
Set in blunt wing, skimmed screaming on ahead.
She followed him. A murrey squirrel eyed
Her warily, cocked upon tail-plumed haunch,
Then, skipping the whirligig of last-year leaves,
Whisked himself out of sight and reappeared
Leering about the bole of a young beech ;
And every time she thought to corner him
He scrambled round on little scratchy hands
To peek at her about the other side.
She lost him, bolting branch to branch, at last —
The impudent brat ! But still high overhead
Flight on exuberant flight of opal scud,
Or of dissolving mist, florid as flame,

Scattered in ecstasy over the blue. And she
Followed, first walking, giving her bright locks
To the cold fervour of the springtime gale,
Whose rush bore the cloud shadow past the cloud
Over the irised wastes of emerald turf.
And still the huge wind volleyed. Save the gulls,
Goldenly in the sunny blast careering
Or on blue-shadowed underwing at plunge,
None shared with her who now could not but run
The splendour and tumult of th' onrushing spring.

And now she ran no more : the gale gave plumes.
One with the shadows whirled along the grass,
One with the onward smother of veering gulls,
One with the pursuit of cloud after cloud,
Swept she. Pure speed coursed in immortal limbs ;
Nostrils drank as from wells of unknown air ;
Ears received the smooth silence of racing floods ;
Light as of glassy suns froze in her eyes ;
Space was given her and she ruled all space.

Spring, author of twifold loveliness,
Who flittest in the mirth of the wild folk,
Profferest greeting in the faces of flowers,
Blowest in the firmamental glory,
Renewest in the heart of the sad human
All faiths, guard thou the innocent spirit
Into whose unknowing hands this noontide
Thou pourest treasure, yet scarce recognised,
That unashamed before man's glib wisdom,
Unabashed beneath the wrath of chance,
She accept in simplicity of homage
The hidden holiness, the created emblem
To be in her, until death shall take her,
The source and secret of eternal spring.

Robert
Nichols

THE STRANGER

Never am I so alone
  As when I walk among the crowd—
Blurred masks of stern or grinning stone,
  Unmeaning eyes and voices loud.

Gaze dares not encounter gaze, . . .
  Humbled, I turn my head aside ;
When suddenly there is a face . . .
  Pale, subdued and grievous-eyed.

Ah, I know that visage meek,
  Those trembling lips, the eyes that shine
But turn from that which they would seek
  With an air piteous, divine !

There is not a line or scar,
  Seal of a sorrow or disgrace,
But I know like sigils are
  Burned in my heart and on my face.

Speak ! O speak ! Thou art the one !
  But thou hast passed with sad head bowed ;
And never am I so alone
  As when I walk among the crowd.

' O NIGHTINGALE MY HEART '

Robert
Nichols

O Nightingale my heart
How sad thou art !
How heavy is thy wing,
Desperately whirrëd that thy throat may fling
Song to the tingling silences remote !
Thine eye whose ruddy spark
Burned fiery of late,
How dead and dark !
Why so soon didst thou sing,
And with such turbulence of love and hate ?

Learn that there is no singing yet can bring
The expected dawn more near ;
And thou art spent already, though the night
Scarce has begun ;
What voice, what eyes wilt thou have for the light
When the light shall appear,
And O what wings to bear thee t'ward the Sun ?

Robert
Nichols

THE PILGRIM

Put by the sun my joyful soul,
We are for darkness that is whole ;

Put by the wine, now for long years
We must be thirsty with salt tears ;

Put by the rose, bind thou instead
The fiercest thorns about thy head ;

Put by the courteous tire, we need
But the poor pilgrim's blackest weed ;

Put by—a'beit with tears—thy lute,
Sing but to God or else be mute.

Take leave of friends save such as dare
Thy love with Loneliness to share.

It is full tide. Put by regret.
Turn, turn away. Forget. Forget.

Put by the sun my lightless soul,
We are for darkness that is whole.

J. D. C. PELLOW

THE TEMPLE

J.D.C.
Pellow

Between the erect and solemn trees
I will go down upon my knees ;
    I shall not find this day
    So meet a place to pray.

Haply the beauty of this place
May work in me an answering grace,
    The stillness of the air
    Be echoed in my prayer.

The worshipping trees arise and run,
With never a swerve, towards the sun ;
    So may my soul's desire
    Turn to its central fire.

With single aim they seek the light,
And scarce a twig in all their height
    Breaks out until the head
    In glory is outspread.

How strong each pillared trunk ; the bark
That covers them, how smooth ; and hark,
    The sweet and gentle voice
    With which the leaves rejoice !

May a like strength and sweetness fill
Desire, and thought, and steadfast will,
    When I remember these
    Fair sacramental trees !

SIEGFRIED SASSOON

SICK LEAVE

Siegfried
Sassoon

When I'm asleep, dreaming and lulled and warm,—
They come, the homeless ones, the noiseless dead.
While the dim charging breakers of the storm
Bellow and drone and rumble overhead,
Out of the gloom they gather about my bed.
    They whisper to my heart ; their thoughts are mine.
    ' Why are you here with all your watches ended ?
    From Ypres to Frise we sought you in the Line.'
In bitter safety I awake, unfriended ;
And while the dawn begins with slashing rain
I think of the Battalion in the mud.
' When are you going out to them again ?
Are they not still your brothers through our blood ? '

Siegfried
Sassoon

I am banished from the patient men who fight.
They smote my heart to pity, built my pride.
Shoulder to aching shoulder, side by side,
They trudged away from life's broad wealds of light.
Their wrongs were mine ; and ever in my sight
They went arrayed in honour. But they died,—
Not one by one : and mutinous I cried
To those who sent them out into the night.

The darkness tells how vainly I have striven
To free them from the pit where they must dwell
In outcast gloom convulsed and jagged and riven
By grappling guns. Love drove me to rebel.
Love drives me back to grope with them through hell ;
And in their tortured eyes I stand forgiven.

REPRESSION OF WAR EXPERIENCE Siegfried Sassoon

Now light the candles ; one ; two ; there's a moth ;
What silly beggars they are to blunder in
And scorch their wings with glory, liquid flame—
No, no, not that,—it's bad to think of war,
When thoughts you've gagged all day come back to
    scare you ;
And it's been proved that soldiers don't go mad
Unless they lose control of ugly thoughts
That drive them out to jabber among the trees.

Now light your pipe ; look, what a steady hand.
Draw a deep breath ; stop thinking ; count fifteen,
And you're as right as rain. . . .
                Why won't it rain ? . . .
I wish there'd be a thunderstorm to-night,
With bucketsful of water to sluice the dark,
And make the roses hang their dripping heads.

Books ; what a jolly company they are,
Standing so quiet and patient on their shelves,
Dressed in dim brown, and black, and white, and green,
And every kind of colour. Which will you read ?
Come on ; O *do* read something ; they're so wise.
I tell you all the wisdom of the world
Is waiting for you on those shelves ; and yet
You sit and gnaw your nails, and let your pipe out,
And listen to the silence : on the ceiling
There's one big, dizzy moth that bumps and flutters ;
And in the breathless air outside the house
The garden waits for something that delays.
There must be crowds of ghosts among the trees,—
Not people killed in battle,—they're in France,—

Siegfried
Sassoon

But horrible shapes in shrouds—old men who died
Slow, natural deaths,—old men with ugly souls,
Who wore their bodies out with nasty sins.

*   *   *   *

You're quiet and peaceful, summering safe at home ;
You'd never think there was a bloody war on ! . . .
O yes, you would . . . why, you can hear the guns.
Hark ! Thud, thud, thud,—quite soft . . . they never
        cease—
Those whispering guns—O Christ, I want to go out
And screech at them to stop—I'm going crazy ;
I'm going stark, staring mad because of the guns.

DOES IT MATTER

Siegfried
Sassoon

Does it matter ?—losing your legs ? . . .
For people will always be kind,
And you need not show that you mind
When the others come in after hunting
To gobble their muffins and eggs.

Does it matter ?—losing your sight ? . . .
There's such splendid work for the blind ;
And people will always be kind,
As you sit on the terrace remembering
And turning your face to the light.

Do they matter ?—those dreams from the pit ? . . .
You can drink and forget and be glad,
And people won't say that you're mad ;
For they'll know that you've fought for your country,
And no one will worry a bit.

Siegfried
Sassoon

CONCERT PARTY

(Egyptian Base Camp).

They are gathering round . . .
Out of the twilight ; over the grey-blue sand,
Shoals of low-jargoning men drift inward to the sound—
The jangle and throb of a piano . . . tum-ti-tum . . .
Drawn by a lamp, they come
Out of the glimmering lines of their tents, over the
     shuffling sand.

O sing us the songs, the songs of our own land,
You warbling ladies in white.
Dimness conceals the hunger in our faces,
This wall of faces risen out of the night,
These eyes that keep their memories of the places
So long beyond their sight.

Jaded and gay, the ladies sing ; and the chap in brown
Tilts his grey hat ; jaunty and lean and pale,
He rattles the keys . . . Some actor-bloke from town . . .
God send you home ; and then *A long, long trail ;*
I hear you calling me ; and *Dixieland.* . . .
Sing slowly . . . now the chorus . . . one by one
We hear them, drink them ; till the concert's done.
Silent, I watch the shadowy mass of soldiers stand.
Silent, they drift away, over the glimmering sand.

KANTARA, *April,* 1918.

134

SONGBOOKS OF THE WAR

Siegfried
Sassoon

In fifty years, when peace outshines
Remembrance of the battle lines,
Adventurous lads will sigh and cast
Proud looks upon the plundered past.
On summer morn or winter's night,
Their hearts will kindle for the fight,
Reading a snatch of soldier-song,
Savage and jaunty, fierce and strong ;
And through the angry marching rhymes
Of blind regret and haggard mirth,
They'll envy us the dazzling times
When sacrifice absolved our earth.

Some ancient man with silver locks
Will lift his weary face to say :
' War was a fiend who stopped our clocks
Although we met him grim and gay.'
And then he'll speak of Haig's last drive,
Marvelling that any came alive
Out of the shambles that men built
And smashed, to cleanse the world of guilt.
But the boys, with grin and sidelong glance,
Will think, ' Poor grandad's day is done.'
And dream of those who fought in France
And lived in time to share the fun.

Siegfried
Sassoon

I watch you, gazing at me from the wall,
And wonder how you'd match your dreams with mine,
If, mastering time's illusion, I could call
You back to share this quiet candle-shine.

For you were young, three hundred years ago ;
And by your looks I guess that you were wise . . .
Come, whisper soft, and Death will never know
You've slipped away from those calm, painted eyes.

Strange is your voice . . . Poor ninny, dead so long,
And all your pride forgotten like your name.
' *One April morn I heard a blackbird's song,*
And joy was in my heart like leaves aflame.'

And so you died before your songs took wing ;
While Andrew Marvell followed in your wake.
' *Love thrilled me into music. I could sing*
But for a moment,—but for beauty's sake.'

Who passes ? There's a star-lit breeze that stirs
The glimmer of white lilies in the gloom.
Who speaks ? Death has his silent messengers.
And there was more than silence in this room

While you were gazing at me from the wall
And wondering how you'd match your dreams with
        mine,
If, mastering time's illusion, you could call
Me back to share your vanished candle-shine.

THRUSHES

Siegfried
Sassoon

Tossed on the glittering air they soar and skim,
Whose voices make the emptiness of light
A windy palace. Quavering from the brim
Of dawn, and bold with song at edge of night,
They clutch their leafy pinnacles and sing
Scornful of man, and from his toils aloof
Whose heart's a haunted woodland whispering ;
Whose thoughts return on tempest-baffled wing ;
Who hears the cry of God in everything,
And storms the gate of nothingness for proof.

Siegfried
Sassoon

Everyone suddenly burst out singing ;
And I was filled with such delight
As prisoned birds must find in freedom,
Winging wildly across the white
Orchards and dark-green fields ; on—on—and out of
    sight.

Everyone's voice was suddenly lifted ;
And beauty came like the setting sun :
My heart was shaken with tears ; and horror
Drifted away . . . O, but Everyone
Was a bird ; and the song was wordless ; the singing
    will never be done.

EDWARD SHANKS

A NIGHT-PIECE

Edward
Shanks

Come out and walk. The last few drops of light
Drain silently out of the cloudy blue ;
The trees are full of the dark-stooping night,
   The fields are wet with dew.

All's quiet in the wood but, far away,
Down the hillside and out across the plain,
Moves, with long trail of white that marks its way,
   The softly panting train.

Come through the clearing. Hardly now we see
The flowers, save dark or light against the grass,
Or glimmering silver on a scented tree
   That trembles as we pass.

Hark now ! So far, so far . . . that distant song . . .
Move not the rustling grasses with your feet.
The dusk is full of sounds, that all along
   The muttering boughs repeat.

So far, so faint, we lift our heads in doubt.
Wind, or the blood that beats within our ears,
Has feigned a dubious and delusive note,
   Such as a dreamer hears.

Again . . . again ! The faint sounds rise and fail.
So far the enchanted tree, the song so low . . .
A drowsy thrush ? A waking nightingale ?
   Silence. We do not know.

Edward
Shanks

My lovely one, be near to me to-night.
For now I need you most, since I have gone
Through the sparse woodland in the fading light,
Where in time past we two have walked alone,
Heard the loud nightjar spin his pleasant note,
And seen the wild rose folded up for sleep,
And whispered, though the soft word choked my
    throat,
Your dear name out across the valley deep.
Be near to me, for now I need you most.
To-night I saw an unsubstantial flame
Flickering along those shadowy paths, a ghost
That turned to me and answered to your name,
Mocking me with a wraith of far delight.
. . . My lovely one, be near to me to-night.

THE GLOW-WORM

The pale road winds faintly upward into the dark skies,
And beside it on the rough grass that the wind invisibly
    stirs,
Sheltered by sharp-speared gorse and the berried juni-
    pers,
Shining steadily with a green light, the glow-worm lies.

We regard it ; and this hill and all the other hills
That fall in folds to the river, very smooth and steep,
And the hangers and brakes that the darkness thickly
    fills
Fade like phantoms round the light, and night is deep,
    so deep,—

That all the world is emptiness about the still flame,
And we are small shadows standing lost in the huge
    night.
We gather up the glow-worm, stooping with dazzled
    sight,
And carry it to the little enclosed garden whence we
    came,

And place it on the short grass. Then the shadowy
    flowers fade,
The walls waver and melt and the houses disappear
And the solid town trembles into insubstantial shade
Round the light of the burning glow-worm, steady and
    clear.

143

Edward
Shanks

When a great wave disturbs the ocean cold
   And throws the bottom waters to the sky,
   Strange apparitions on the surface lie,
Great battered vessels, stripped of gloss and gold,
And, writhing in their pain, sea-monsters old,
   Who stain the waters with a bloody dye,
   With unaccustomed mouths bellow and cry
And vex the waves with struggling fin and fold.

And with these too come little trivial things
   Tossed from the deeps by the same casual hand ;
   A faint sea flower, dragged from the lowest sand,
That will not undulate its luminous wings
In the slow tides again, lies dead and swings
   Along the muddy ripples to the land.

A HOLLOW ELM

Edward
Shanks

What hast thou not withstood,
   Tempest-despising tree,
Whose bloat and riven wood
   Gapes now so hollowly,
What rains have beaten thee through many years,
What snows from off thy branches dripped like tears ?

Calmly thou standest now
   Upon thy sunny mound ;
The first spring breezes flow
   Past with sweet dizzy sound ;
Yet on thy pollard top the branches few
Stand stiffly out, disdain to murmur too.

The children at thy foot
   Open new-lighted eyes,
Where, on gnarled bark and root,
   The soft warm sunshine lies—
Dost thou, upon thine ancient sides, resent
The touch of youth, quick and impermanent ?

These at the beck of spring
   Live in the moment still :
Thy boughs unquivering,
   Remembering winter's chill,
And many other winters past and gone,
Are mocked, not cheated, by the transient sun.

Hast thou so much withstood,
   Tempest-despising tree,
That now thy hollow wood
   Stiffens disdainfully
Against the soft spring airs and soft spring rain,
Knowing too well that winter comes again ?

FÊTE GALANTE;

THE TRIUMPH OF LOVE

Aristonoë, the fading shepherdess,
Gathers the young girls round her in a ring,
Teaching them wisdom of love,
What to say, how to dress,
How frown, how smile,
How suitors to their dancing feet to bring,
How in mere walking to beguile,
What words cunningly said in what a way
Will draw man's busy fancy astray,
All the alphabet, grammar and syntax of love.

The garden smells are sweet,
Daisies spring in the turf under the high-heeled feet,
Dense, dark banks of laurel grow
Behind the wavering row
Of golden, flaxen, black, brown, auburn heads,
Behind the light and shimmering dresses
Of these unreal, modern shepherdesses ;
And gaudy flowers in formal patterned beds
Vary the dim long vistas of the park,
Far as the eye can see,
Till at the forest's edge the ground grows dark
And the flowers vanish in the obscurity.

The young girls gather round her,
Remembering eagerly how their fathers found her
Fresh as a spring-like wind in February,
Subtler in her moving heart than sun-motes that vary
At every waft of an opening and shutting door ;
They gather chattering near,

146

Hush, break out in laughter, whisper aside,   Edward
Grow silent more and more,   Shanks
Though she will never chide.
Now through the silence sounds her voice still clear,
And all give ear.
Like a silver thread through the golden afternoon,
Equably the voice discloses
All that age-old wisdom ; like an endless tune
Aristonoë's voice wavers among the roses,
Level and unimpassioned,
Telling them how of nothing love is fashioned,
How it is but a movement of the mind,
Bidding Celia mark
That light skirts fluttering in the wind,
Or white flowers stuck in dark
Glistening hair, have fired the dull beholder,
Or telling Anais
That faint indifference ere now hath bred a kiss
Denied to flaunted snowy breast or shoulder.

The girls attend,
Each thinking on her friend,
Whether he be real or imaginary,
Whether he be loving or cold ;
For each ere she grows old
Means to pursue her joy, and the whole unwary
Troop of their wishes has this wild quarry in cry,
That draws them ineluctably,
More and more as the summer slippeth by.
And Celia leans aside
To contemplate her black-silked ankle on the grass ;
In remote dreaming pride,
Rosalind recalls the image in her glass ;
Phillis through all her body feels

How divine energy steals,
Quiescent power and resting speed,
Stretches her arms out, feels the warm blood run
Ready for pursuit, for strife and deed,
And turns her glowing face up to the sun.
Phillida smiles,
And lazily trusts her lazy wit,
A slow arrow that hath often hit ;
Chloe, bemused by many subtle wiles,
Grows not more dangerous for all of it,
But opens her red lips, yawning drowsily,
And shows her small white teeth,
Dimpling the round chin beneath,
And stretches, moving her young body deliciously.

And still the lesson goes on,
For this is an old story that is never done ;
And now the precept is of ribbon and shoe,
What with linens and silks love finds to do,
And how man's heart is tangled in a string
Or taken in gauze like a weak and helpless thing.
Chloe falls asleep ; and the long summer day
Drifts slowly past the girls and the warm roses,
Giving in dreams its hours away.
Now Stella throws her head back, and Phillis disposes
Her strong brown hands quietly in her lap,
And Rose's slender feet grow restless and tap
The turf to an imaginary tune.
Now all this grace of youthful bodies and faces
Is wrought to a glow by the golden weather of June ;
Now, Love, completing grace of all the graces,
Strong in these hearts thy pure streams rise,
Transmuting what they learn by heavenly alchemies.
Swift from the listeners the spell vanishes,

And through the tinkling, empty words,
True thoughts of true love press,
Flying and wheeling nearer ;
As through a sunny sky a flock of birds
Against the throbbing blue grows clearer and clearer,
So closer come these thoughts and dearer.

Edward
Shanks

Helen rises with a laugh ;
Chloe wakes ;
All the enchantment scatters off like chaff ;
The cord is loosened and the spell breaks.
Rosalind
Resolves that to-night she will be kind to her lover,
Unreflecting, warm and kind.
Celia tells the lessons over,
Counting on her fingers—one and two . . .
Ribbon and shoe,
Skirts, flowers, song, dancing, laughter, eyes . . .
Through the whole catalogue of formal gallantry
And studious coquetries,
Counting to herself maliciously.

But the old, the fading shepherdess, Aristonoë,
Rises stiffly and walks alone
Down the broad path where densely the laurels grow,
And over a little lawn, not closely mown,
Where wave the flowering grass and the rich meadow-
She seems to walk painfully now and slow,   [sweet.
And drags a little on her high-heeled feet.
She stops at last below
An old and twisted plum-tree, whose last petal is gone,
Leans on the comfortable, rugged bole,
And stares through the green leaves at the drooping sun.
The tree and the warm light comfort her ageing soul.

149

<table>
<tr><td>Edward
Shanks</td><td>On the other lawn behind her, out of sight,
The girls at play
Drive out melancholy by lively delight,
And the wind carries their songs and laughter away.</td></tr>
</table>

Some begin dancing and seriously tread
A modern measure up and down the grass,
Turn, slide with bending knees, and pass
With dipping hand and poising head,
Float through the sun in pairs, like newly shed
And golden leaves astray
Upon the warm wind of an autumn day,
When the Indian summer rules the air.
Others, having found,
Lying idly on the sun-hot ground,
Shuttlecocks and battledores,
Play with the buoyant feathers and stare
Dazzled at the plaything as it soars,
Vague against the shining sky,
Where light yet throbs and confuses the eye,
Then see it again, white and clear,
As slowly, poisèdly it falls by
The dark green foliage and floats near.
But Celia, apart, is pensive and must sigh,
And Anais but faintly pursues the game.
An encroaching, inner flame
Burns in their hearts with the acrid smoke of unrest ;
But gaiety runs like quicksilver in Rose's breast,
And Phillis, rising,
Walks by herself with high and springy tread,
All her young blood racing from heels to head,
Breeding new desires and a new surprising
Strength and determination,
Whereof are bred
Confidence and joy and exultation.

The long day closes ;   Edward
Rosalind's hour draws near, and Chloe's and Rose's,   Shanks
The hour that Celia has prayed,
The hour for which Anais and Stella have stayed,
When Helen shall forget her wit,
And Phillida by a sure arrow at length be hit,
And Phillis, the fleet runner, be at length overtaken ;
When this bough of young blossoms
By the rough, eager gatherers shall be shaken.
Their eyes grow dim,
Their hearts flutter like taken birds in their bosoms,
As the light dies out of heaven,
And a faint, delicious tremor runs through every limb,
And faster the volatile blood through their veins is
    driven.

The long day closes ;
The last light fades in the amber sky ;
Warm through the warm dusk glow the roses,
And a heavier shade drops slowly from the trees,
While through the garden as all colours die
The scents come livelier on the quickening breeze.
The world grows larger, vaguer, dimmer,
Over the dark laurels a few faint stars glimmer ;
The moon, that was a pallid ghost,
Hung low on the horizon, faint and lost,
Comes up, a full and splendid golden round
By black and sharp-cut foliage overcrossed.
The girls laugh and whisper now with hardly a sound
Till all sound vanishes, dispersed in the night,
Like a wisp of cloud that fades in the moon's light,
And the garden grows silent and the shadows grow
Deeper and blacker below
The mysteriously moving and murmuring trees,

That stand out darkly against the star-luminous
    sky ;
Huge stand the trees,
Shadowy, whispering immensities,
That rain down quietude and darkness on heart and
    eye.
None move, none speak, none sigh·
But from the laurels comes a leaping voice
Crying in tones that seem not man's nor boy's,
But only joy's,
And hard behind a loud tumultuous crying,
A tangled skein of noise,
And the girls see their lovers come, each vying
Against the next in glad and confident poise,
Or softly moving
To the side of the chosen with gentle words and loving
Gifts for her pleasure of sweetmeats and jewelled
    toys.

Dear Love, whose strength no pedantry can stir,
Whether in thine iron enemies,
Or in thine own strayed follower
Bemused with subtleties and sophistries,
Now dost thou rule the garden, now
The gatherers' hands have grasped the scented bough.

Slow the sweet hours resolve, and one by one are
    sped.
The garden lieth empty. Overhead
A nightjar rustles by, wing touching wing,
And passes, uttering
His hoarse and whirring note.
The daylight birds long since are fled,
Nor has the moon yet touched the brown bird's throat.

152

All's quiet, all is silent, all around   Edward
The day's heat rises gently from the ground,   Shanks
And still the broad moon travels up the sky,
Now glancing through the trees and now so high
That all the garden through her rays are shed,
And from the laurels one can just descry
Where in the distance looms enormously
The old house, with all its windows black and dead.

SONG

As I lay in the early sun,
Stretched in the grass, I thought upon
My true love, my dear love,
Who has my heart for ever,
Who is my happiness when we meet,
My sorrow when we sever.
She is all fire when I do burn,
Gentle when I moody turn,
Brave when I am sad and heavy
And all laughter when I am merry.
And so I lay and dreamed and dreamed,
And so the day wheeled on,
While all the birds with thoughts like mine
Were singing to the sun.

FREDEGOND SHOVE

A DREAM IN EARLY SPRING

Fredegond
Shove

Now when I sleep the thrush breaks through my dreams
With sharp reminders of the coming day :
After his call, one minute I remain
Unwaked, and on the darkness which is Me
There springs the image of a daffodil,
Growing upon a grassy bank alone,
And seeming with great joy his bell to fill
With drops of golden dew, which on the lawn
He shakes again, where they lie bright and chill.

His head is drooped ; the shrouded winds that sing
Bend him which way they will : never on earth
Was there before so beautiful a ghost.
Alas ! he had a less than flower-birth,
And like a ghost indeed must shortly glide
From all but the sad cells of memory,
Where he will linger, an imprisoned beam,
Or fallen shadow of the golden world,
Long after this and many another dream.

THE WORLD

I wish this world and its green hills were mine,
But it is not ; the wandering shepherd star
Is not more distant, gazing from afar
On the unreapèd pastures of the sea,
Than I am from the world, the world from me.
At night the stars on milky way that shine
Seem things one might possess, but this round green
Is for the cows that rest, these and the sheep :
To them the slopes and pastures offer sleep ;
My sleep I draw from the far fields of blue,
Whence cold winds come and go among the few
Bright stars we see and many more unseen.

Birds sing on earth all day among the flowers,
Taking no thought of any other thing
But their own hearts, for out of them they sing :
Their songs are kindred to the blossom heads,
Faint as the petals which the blackthorn sheds,
And like the earth—not alien songs as ours.
To them this greenness and this island peace
Are life and death and happiness in one ;
Nor are they separate from the white sun,
Or those warm winds which nightly wash the deep
Or starlight in the valleys, or new sleep ;
And from these things they ask for no release.

But we can never call this world our own,
Because we long for it, and yet we know
That should the great winds call us, we should go ;
Should they come calling out across the cold,
We should rise up and leave the sheltered fold
And follow the great road to the unknown.

We should pass by the barns and haystacks brown, Fredegond
Should leave the wild pool and the nightingale ; Shove
Across the ocean we should set a sail
And, coming to the world's pale brim, should fly
Out to the very middle of the sky,
On past the moon ; nor should we once look down.

' And he, casting away his garment, rose and came to Jesus.'

And he cast it down, down, on the green grass,
Over the young crocuses, where the dew was—
He cast the garment of his flesh that was full of death,
And like a sword his spirit showed out of the cold sheath.

He went a pace or two, he went to meet his Lord,
And, as I said, his spirit looked like a clean sword,
And seeing him the naked trees began shivering,
And all the birds cried out aloud as it were late spring.

And the Lord came on, He came down, and saw
That a soul was waiting there for Him, one without flaw,
And they embraced in the churchyard where the robins
    play,
And the daffodils hang down their heads, as they burn
    away.

The Lord held his head fast, and you could see
That he kissed the unsheathed ghost that was gone
    free—
As a hot sun, on a March day, kisses the cold ground ;
And the spirit answered, for he knew well that his peace
    was found.

The spirit trembled, and sprang up at the Lord's word—
As on a wild, April day, springs a small bird—
So the ghost's feet lifting him up, he kissed the Lord's
    cheek,
And for the greatness of their love neither of them could
    speak.

But the Lord went then, to show him the way,
Over the young crocuses, under the green may
That was not quite in flower yet—to a far-distant land;
And the ghost followed, like a naked cloud holding the
    sun's hand.

Fredegond
Shove

Fredegond Shove A MAN DREAMS THAT HE IS THE CREATOR

I sat in heaven like the sun
  Above a storm when winter was :
  I took the snowflakes one by one
And turned their fragile shapes to glass :
I washed the rivers blue with rain
And made the meadows green again.

I took the birds and touched their springs,
  Until they sang unearthly joys :
They flew about on golden wings
  And glittered like an angel's toys :
I filled the fields with flowers' eyes,
As white as stars in Paradise.

And then I looked on man and knew
  Him still intent on death—still proud ;
Whereat into a rage I flew
  And turned my body to a cloud :
In the dark shower of my soul
The star of earth was swallowed whole.

J. C. SQUIRE

RIVERS

J. C.
Squire

Rivers I have seen which were beautiful,
Slow rivers winding in the flat fens,
With bands of reeds like thronged green swords
   Guarding the mirrored sky ;
And streams down-tumbling from the chalk hills
To valleys of meadows and watercress-beds,
And bridges whereunder, dark weed-coloured shadows,
   Trout flit or lie.

I know those rivers that peacefully glide
Past old towers and shaven gardens,
Where mottled walls rise from the water
   And mills all streaked with flour ;
And rivers with wharves and rusty shipping,
That flow with a stately tidal motion
Towards their destined estuaries
   Full of the pride of power ;

Noble great rivers, Thames and Severn,
Tweed with his gateway of many grey arches,
Clyde, dying at sunset westward
   In a sea as red as blood ;
Rhine and his hills in close procession,
Placid Elbe, Seine slaty and swirling,
And Isar, son of the Alpine snows,
   A furious turquoise flood.

All these I have known, and with slow eyes
I have walked on their shores and watched them,
And softened to their beauty and loved them
   Wherever my feet have been ;

And a hundred others also
Whose names long since grew into me,
That, dreaming in light or darkness,
    I have seen, though I have not seen.

Those rivers of thought : cold Ebro,
And blue racing Guadiana,
Passing white houses, high-balconied
    That ache in a sun-baked land,
Congo, and Nile and Colorado,
Niger, Indus, Zambesi,
And the Yellow River, and the Oxus,
    And the river that dies in sand.

What splendours are theirs, what continents,
What tribes of men, what basking plains,
Forests and lion-hided deserts,
    Marshes, ravines and falls :
All hues and shapes and tempers
Wandering they take as they wander
From those far springs that endlessly
    The far sea calls.

O in reverie I know the Volga
That turns his back upon Europe,
And the two great cities on his banks,
    Novgorod and Astrakhan ;
Where the world is a few soft colours,
And under the dove-like evening
The boatmen chant ancient songs,
    The tenderest known to man.

And the holy river Ganges,
His fretted cities veiled in moonlight,

166

Arches and buttresses silver-shadowy
    In the high moon,
And palms grouped in the moonlight
And fanes girdled with cypresses,
Their domes of marble softly shining
    To the high silver moon.

J. C.
Squire

And that aged Brahmapootra
Who beyond the white Himalayas
Passes many a lamassery
    On rocks forlorn and frore,
A block of gaunt grey stone walls
With rows of little barred windows,
Where shrivelled young monks in yellow silk
    Are hidden for evermore. . . .

But O that great river, the Amazon,
I have sailed up its gulf with eyelids closed,
And the yellow waters tumbled round,
    And all was rimmed with sky,
Till the banks drew in, and the trees' heads,
And the lines of green grew higher
And I breathed deep, and there above me
    The forest wall stood high.

Those forest walls of the Amazon
Are level under the blazing blue
And yield no sound but the whistles and shrieks
    Of the swarming bright macaws ;
And under their lowest drooping boughs
Mud-banks torpidly bubble,
And the water drifts, and logs in the water
    Drift and twist and pause.

167

J. C.
Squire

And everywhere, tacitly joining,
Float noiseless tributaries,
Tall avenues paved with water :
    And as I silent fly
The vegetation like a painted scene,
Spars and spikes and monstrous fans
And ferns from hairy sheaths up-springing,
    Evenly passes by.

And stealthier stagnant channels
Under low niches of drooping leaves
Coil into deep recesses :
    And there have I entered, there
To heavy, hot, dense, dim places
Where creepers climb and sweat and climb,
And the drip and splash of oozing water
    Loads the stifling air.

Rotting scrofulous steaming trunks,
Great horned emerald beetles crawling,
Ants and huge slow butterflies
    That had strayed and lost the sun ;
Ah, sick I have swooned as the air thickened
To a pallid brown ecliptic glow,
And on the forest, fallen with languor,
    Thunder has begun.

Thunder in the dun dusk, thunder
Rolling and battering and cracking,
The caverns shudder with a terrible glare
    Again and again and again,
Till the land bows in the darkness,
Utterly lost and defenceless,
Smitten and blinded and overwhelmed
    By the crashing rods of rain.

And then in the forests of the Amazon,
When the rain has ended, and silence come,
What dark luxuriance unfolds
   From behind the night's drawn bars :
The wreathing odours of a thousand trees
And the flowers' faint gleaming presences,
And over the clearings and the still waters
   Soft indigo and hanging stars.

J. C.
Squire

*   *   *   *

O many and many are rivers,
And beautiful are all rivers,
And lovely is water everywhere
   That leaps or glides or stays ;
Yet by starlight, moonlight, or sunlight,
Long, long though they look, these wandering eyes,
Even on the fairest waters of dream,
   Never untroubled gaze.

For whatever stream I stand by,
And whatever river I dream of,
There is something still in the back of my mind
   From very far away ;
There is something I saw and see not,
A country full of rivers
That stirs in my heart and speaks to me
   More sure, more dear than they.

And always I ask and wonder
(Though often I do not know it) :
Why does this water not smell like water ?
   Where is the moss that grew
Wet and dry on the slabs of granite
And the round stones in clear brown water ?
—And a pale film rises before them
   Of the rivers that first I knew.

J. C.
Squire

Though famous are the rivers of the great world,
Though my heart from those alien waters drinks
Delight however pure from their loveliness,
   And awe however deep,
Would I wish for a moment the miracle,
That those waters should come to Chagford,
Or gather and swell in Tavy Cleave
   Where the stones cling to the steep ?

No, even were they Ganges and Amazon
In all their great might and majesty,
League upon league of wonders,
   I would lose them all, and more,
For a light chiming of small bells,
A twisting flash in the granite,
The tiny thread of a pixie waterfall
   That lives by Vixen Tor.

Those rivers in that lost country,
They were brown as a clear brown bead is,
Or red with the earth that rain washed down,
   Or white with china-clay ;
And some tossed foaming over boulders,
And some curved mild and tranquil,
In wooded vales securely set
   Under the fond warm day.

Okement and Erme and Avon,
Exe and his ruffled shallows,
I could cry as I think of those rivers
   That knew my morning dreams ;
The weir by Tavistock at evening
When the circling woods were purple,
And the Lowman in spring with the lent-lilies,
   And the little moorland streams.

170

For many a hillside streamlet
There falls with a broken tinkle,
Falling and dying, falling and dying,
    In little cascades and pools,
Where the world is furze and heather
And flashing plovers and fixed larks,
And an empty sky, whitish blue,
    That small world rules.

There, there, where the high waste bog-lands
And the drooping slopes and the spreading valleys,
The orchards and the cattle-sprinkled pastures
    Those travelling musics fill,
There is my lost Abana,
And there is my nameless Pharphar
That mixed with my heart when I was a boy,
    And time stood still.

And I say I will go there and die there :
But I do not go there, and sometimes
I think that the train could not carry me there,
    And it's possible, maybe,
That it's farther than Asia or Africa,
Or any voyager's harbour,
Farther, farther, beyond recall. . . .
    O even in memory !

J. C.
Squire

EPITAPH IN OLD MODE

The leaves fall gently on the grass,
And all the willow trees and poplar trees and elder trees
That bend above her where she sleeps,
O all the willow trees, the willow trees
Breathe sighs above her tomb.

O pause and pity as you pass.
She loved so tenderly, so quietly, so hopelessly ;
And sometimes comes one here and weeps—
She loved so tenderly, so tenderly,
And never told them whom.

SONNET

J. C.
Squire

There was an Indian, who had known no change,
  Who strayed content along a sunlit beach
Gathering shells. He heard a sudden strange
  Commingled noise : looked up ; and gasped for
     speech.
For in the bay, where nothing was before,
  Moved on the sea, by magic, huge canoes,
With bellying cloths on poles, and not one oar,
  And fluttering coloured signs and clambering crews.

And he, in fear, this naked man alone,
  His fallen hands forgetting all their shells,
His lips gone pale, knelt low behind a stone,
  And stared, and saw, and did not understand,
  Columbus's doom-burdened caravels
    Slant to the shore, and all their seamen land.

Within mankind's duration, so they say,
Khephren and Ninus lived but yesterday.
Asia had no name till man was old
And long had learned the use of iron and gold ;
And æons had passed, when the first corn was planted,
Since first the use of syllables was granted.

Men were on earth while climates slowly swung,
Fanning wide zones to heat and cold, and long
Subsidence turned great continents to sea,
And seas dried up, dried up interminably,
Age after age ; enormous seas were dried
Amid wastes of land. And the last monsters died.

Earth wore another face. O since that prime
Man with how many works has sprinkled time !
Hammering, hewing, digging tunnels, roads ;
Building ships, temples, multiform abodes.
How, for his body's appetites, his toils
Have conquered all earth's products, all her soils;
And in what thousand thousand shapes of art
He has tried to find a language for his heart !

Never at rest, never content or tired :
Insatiate wanderer, marvellously fired,
Most grandly piling and piling into the air
Stones that will topple or arch he knows not where.

And yet did I, this spring, think it more strange,
More grand, more full of awe, than all that change,
And lovely and sweet and touching unto tears,
That through man's chronicled and unchronicled years,

And even into that unguessable beyond
The water-hen has nested by a pond,
Weaving dry flags, into a beaten floor,
The one sure product of her only lore.
Low on a ledge above the shadowed water
Then, when she heard no men, as nature taught her,
Plashing around with busy scarlet bill
She built that nest, her nest, and builds it still.

O let your strong imagination turn
The great wheel backward, until Troy unburn,
And then unbuild, and seven Troys below
Rise out of death, and dwindle, and outflow,
Till all have passed, and none has yet been there :
Back, ever back. Our birds still crossed the air ;
Beyond our myriad changing generations
Still built, unchanged, their known inhabitations.
A million years before Atlantis was
Our lark sprang from some hollow in the grass,
Some old soft hoof-print in a tussock's shade ;
And the wood-pigeon's smooth snow-white eggs were
    laid,
High, amid green pines' sunset-coloured shafts,
And rooks their villages of twiggy rafts
Set on the tops of elms, where elms grew then,
And still the thumbling tit and perky wren
Popped through the tiny doors of cosy balls
And the blackbird lined with moss his high-built walls ;
A round mud cottage held the thrush's young,
And straws from the untidy sparrow's hung.
And, skimming forktailed in the evening air,
When man first was were not the martens there ?
Did not those birds some human shelter crave,
And stow beneath the cornice of his cave

Their dry tight cups of clay ? And from each door
Peeped on a morning wiseheads three or four.

Yes, daw and owl, curlew and crested hern,
Kingfisher, mallard, water-rail and tern,
Chaffinch and greenfinch, warbler, stonechat, ruff,
Pied wagtail, robin, fly-catcher and chough,
Missel-thrush, magpie, sparrow-hawk, and jay,
Built, those far ages gone, in this year's way.
And the first man who walked the cliffs of Rame,
As I this year, looked down and saw the same
Blotches of rusty red on ledge and cleft
With grey-green spots on them, while right and left
A dizzying tangle of gulls were floating and flying,
Wheeling and crossing and darting, crying and crying,
Circling and crying, over and over and over,
Crying with swoop and hover and fall and recover.
And below on a rock against the grey sea fretted,
Pipe-necked and stationary and silhouetted,
Cormorants stood in a wise, black, equal row
Above the nests and long blue eggs we know.

O delicate chain over all the ages stretched,
O dumb tradition from what far darkness fetched :
Each little architect with its one design
Perpetual, fixed and right in stuff and line,
Each little ministrant who knows one thing,
One learnèd rite to celebrate the spring.
Whatever alters else on sea or shore,
These are unchanging : man must still explore.

W. J. TURNER

SILENCE

W. J.
Turner

It was bright day and all the trees were still
In the deep valley, and the dim Sun glowed ;
The clay in hard-baked fire along the hill
Leapt through dark trunks to apples green and gold,
Smooth, hard and cold, they shone like lamps of stone .

They were bright bubbles bursting from the trees,
Swollen and still among the dark green boughs ;
On their bright skins the shadows of the leaves
Seemed the faint ghosts of summers long since gone,
Faint ghosts of ghosts, the dreams of ghostly eyes.

There was no sound between those breathless hills.
Only the dim Sun hung there, nothing moved ;
The thronged, massed, crowded multitude of leaves
Hung like dumb tongues that loll and gasp for air :
The grass was thick and still, between the trees.

There were big apples lying on the ground,
Shining, quite still, as though they had been stunned
By some great violent spirit stalking through,
Leaving a deep and supernatural calm
Round a dead beetle upturned in a furrow.

A valley filled with dark, quiet, leaf-thick trees,
Loaded with green, cold, faintly shining suns ;
And in the sky a great dim burning disc! —
Madness it is to watch these twisted trunks
And to see nothing move and hear no sound !

Let's make a noise, Hey ! . . . Hey ! . . .Hullo ! Hullo !

KENT IN WAR

The pebbly brook is cold to-night,
  Its water soft as air,
A clear, cold, crystal-bodied wind
  Shadowless and bare,
Leaping and running in this world
  Where dark-horned cattle stare :

Where dark-horned cattle stare, hoof-firm
  On the dark pavements of the sky,
And trees are mummies swathed in sleep
  And small dark hills crowd wearily :
Soft multitudes of snow-grey clouds
  Without a sound march by.

Down at the bottom of the road
  I smell the woody damp
Of that cold spirit in the grass,
  And leave my hill-top camp—
Its long gun pointing in the sky—
  And take the Moon for lamp.

I stop beside the bright cold glint
  Of that thin spirit in the grass,
So gay it is, so innocent !
  I watch its sparkling footsteps pass
Lightly from smooth round stone to stone,
  Hid in the dew-hung grass.

My lamp shines in the globes of dew,
  And leaps into that crystal wind
Running along the shaken grass
  To each dark hole that it can find—

The crystal wind, the Moon my lamp,
  Have vanished in a wood that's blind.

W. J.
Turner

High lies my small, my shadowy camp,
  Crowded about by small dark hills ;
With sudden small white flowers the sky
  Above the woods' dark greenness fills ;
And hosts of dark-browed, muttering trees
  In trance the white Moon stills.

I move among their tall grey forms,
  A thin moon-glimmering, wandering Ghost,
Who takes his lantern through the world
  In search of life that he has lost,
While watching by that long lean gun
  Up on his small hill post.

The mind of the people is like mud,
From which arise strange and beautiful things,
But mud is none the less mud,
Though it bear orchids and prophesying Kings,
Dreams, trees, and water's bright babblings.

It has found form and colour and light,
The cold glimmer of the ice-wrapped Poles ;
It has called a far-off glow Arcturus,
And some pale weeds, lilies of the valley.

It has imagined Virgil, Helen and Cassandra ;
The sack of Troy, and the weeping for Hector—
Rearing stark up 'mid all this beauty
In the thick, dull neck of Ajax.

There is a dark Pine in Lapland,
And the great, figured Horn of the Reindeer,
Moving soundlessly across the snow,
Is its twin brother, double-dreamed,
In the mind of a far-off people.

It is strange that a little mud
Should echo with sounds, syllables, and letters,
Should rise up and call a mountain Popocatapetl,
And a green-leafed wood Oleander.

These are the ghosts of invisible things ;
There is no Lapland, no Helen and no Hector,
And the Reindeer is a darkening of the brain,
And Oleander is but Oleander.

Mary Magdalena and the vine Lachryma Christi W. J. Turner
Were like ghosts up the ghost of Vesuvius,
As I sat and drank wine with the soldiers,
As I sat in the Inn on the mountain,
Watching the shadows in my mind.

The mind of the people is like mud,
Where are the imperishable things,
The ghosts that flicker in the brain—
Silent women, orchids, and prophesying Kings,
Dreams, trees, and water's bright babblings!

W J.
Turner

Gently, sorrowfully sang the maid
   Sowing the ploughed field over,
And her song was only :
   ' Come, O my lover ! '

Strangely, strangely shone the light,
   Stilly wound the river :
' Thy love is a dead man,
   He'll come back never.'

Sadly, sadly passed the maid
The fading dark hills over ;
   Still her song far, far away said :
   ' Come, O my lover ! '

THE PRINCESS

W. J.
Turner

The stone-grey roses by the desert's rim
Are soft-edged shadows on the moonlit sand,
Grey are the broken walls of Khangavar,
That haunt of nightingales, whose voices are
Fountains that bubble in the dream-soft Moon.

Shall the Gazelles with moonbeam pale bright feet
Entering the vanished gardens sniff the air—
Some scent may linger of that ancient time,
Musician's song, or poet's passionate rhyme,
The Princess dead, still wandering love-sick there.

A Princess pale and cold as mountain snow,
In cool, dark chambers sheltered from the sun,
With long dark lashes and small delicate hands :
All Persia sighed to kiss her small red mouth
Until they buried her in shifting sand.

And the Gazelles shall flit by in the Moon
And never shake the frail Tree's lightest leaves,
And moonlight roses perfume the pale Dawn
Until the scarlet life that left her lips
Gathers its shattered beauty in the sky.

PEACE

In low chalk hills the great King's body lay,
And bright streams fell, tinkling like polished tin,
As though they carried off his armoury,
And spread it glinting through his wide domain.

Old bearded soldiers sat and gazed dim-eyed
At the strange brightness flowing under trees,
And saw his sword flashing in ancient battles,
And drank, and swore, and trembled helplessly.

And bright-haired maidens dipped their cold wh
    arms,
And drew them glittering colder, whiter, still ;
The sky sparkled like the dead King's blue eye
Upon the sentries that were dead as trees.

His shining shield lay in an old grey town,
And white swans sailed so still and dreamfully,
They seemed the thoughts of those white, peaceful h
Mirrored that day within his glazing eyes.

And in the square the pale cool butter sold,
Cropped from the daisies sprinkled on the downs,
And old wives cried their wares, like queer day ov
Piercing the old men's sad and foolish dreams.

And Time flowed on till all the realm forgot
The great King lying in the low chalk hills ;
Only the busy water dripping through
His hard white bones knew of him lying there.

DEATH

W. J.
Turner

hen I am dead a few poor souls shall grieve
 I grieved for my brother long ago.
Scarce did my eyes grow dim,
I had forgotten him ;
was far-off hearing the spring winds blow,
And many summers burned
hen, though still reeling with my eyes aflame,
I heard that faded name
hispered one Spring amid the hurrying world
From which, years gone, he turned.

ooked up at my windows and I saw
ie trees, thin spectres sucked forth by the moon.
The air was very still
Above a distant hill ;
was the hour of night's full silver moon.
' O are thou there my brother ? ' my soul cried ;
ıd all the pale stars down bright rivers wept,
As my heart sadly crept
out the empty hills, bathed in that light
That lapped him when he died.

 ! it was cold, so cold ; do I not know
w dead my heart on that remembered day !
Clear in a far-away place
 see his delicate face
t as he called me from my solitary play,
Giving into my hands a tiny tree.
 planted it in the dark, blossomless ground
Gravely, without a sound ;
en back I went and left him standing by
Iis birthday gift to me.

187

W. J.
Turner

In that far land perchance it quietly grows
Drinking the rain, making a pleasant shade ;
    Birds in its branches fly
    Out of the fathomless sky
Where worlds of circling light arise and fade.
    Blindly it quivers in the bright flood of day,
Or drowned in multitudinous shouts of rain
    Glooms o'er the dark-veiled plain—
Buried below, the ghost that's in his bones
    Dreams in the sodden clay.

And, while he faded, drunk with beauty's eyes
I kissed bright girls and laughed deep in dumb trees
    That stared fixt in the air
    Like madmen in despair
Gaped up from earth with the escaping breeze.
    I saw earth's exaltation slowly creep
Out of their myriad sky-embracing veins.
    I laughed along the lanes,
Meeting Death riding in from the hollow seas
    Through black-wreathed woods asleep.

I laughed, I swaggered on the cold hard ground—
Through the grey air trembled a falling wave—
    ' Thou'rt pale, O Death ! ' I cried,
    Mocking him in my pride ;
And passing I dreamed not of that lonely grave,
    But of leaf-maidens whose pale, moon-like hands
Above the tree-foam waved in the icy air,
    Sweeping with shining hair
Through the green-tinted sky, one moment fled
    Out of immortal lands.

188

One windless Autumn night the Moon came out   W. J.
In a white sea of cloud, a field of snow ;   Turner
  In darkness shaped of trees,
  I sank upon my knees
And watched her shining, from the small wood below—
  Faintly Death flickered in an owl's far cry—
We floated soundless in the great gulf of space,
  Her light upon my face—
Immortal, shining in that dark wood I knelt
  And knew I could not die.

And knew I could not die—O Death, didst thou
Heed my vain glory, standing pale by thy dead ?
  There is a spirit who grieves
  Amid earth's dying leaves ;
Was't thou that wept beside my brother's bed ?
  For I did never mourn nor heed at all
Him passing on his temporal elm-wood bier ;
  I never shed a tear.
The drooping sky spread grey-winged through my soul,
  While stones and earth did fall.

That sound rings down the years—I hear it ye.—
All earthly life's a winding funeral—
  And though I never wept,
  But into the dark coach stept,
Dreaming by night to answer the blood's sweet call,
  She who stood there, high-breasted, with small, wise
      lips,
And gave me wine to drink and bread to eat,
  Has not more steadfast feet,
But fades from my arms as fade from mariners' eyes
  The sea's most beauteous ships.

189

W. J.
Turner

The trees and hills of earth were once as close
As my own brother, they are becoming dreams
   And shadows in my eyes ;
   More dimly lies
Guaya deep in my soul, the coastline gleams
   Faintly along the darkening crystalline seas.
Glimmering and lovely still, 'twill one day go ;
   The surging dark will flow
Over my hopes and joys, and blot out all
   Earth's hills and skies and trees.

I shall look up one night and see the Moon
For the last time shining above the hills,
   And thou, silent, wilt ride
   Over the dark hillside.
'Twill be, perchance, the time of daffodils—
   ' *How come those bright immortals in the woods ?*
Their joy being young, didst thou not drag them all
   Into dark graves ere Fall ? '
Shall life thus haunt me, wondering, as I go
   To thy deep solitudes ?

There is a figure with a down-turned torch
Carved on a pillar in an olden time,
   A calm and lovely boy
   Who comes not to destroy
But to lead age back to its golden prime.
   Thus did an antique sculptor draw thee, Death,
With smooth and beauteous brow and faint sweet smile,
   Not haggard, gaunt and vile,
And thou perhaps art thus to whom men may,
   Unvexed, give up their breath.

But in my soul thou sittest like a dream
Among earth's mountains, by her dim-coloured seas;
   A wild unearthly Shape
   In thy dark-glimmering cape,
Piping a tune of wavering melodies,
   Thou sittest, ay, thou sittest at the feast
Of my brief life among earth's bright-wreathed flowers,
   Staining the dancing hours
With sombre gleams until, abrupt, thou risest
   And all, at once, is ceased.

W. J.
Turner

BIBLIOGRAPHY

(Some of these lists, which include poetical works only, are incomplete).

LASCELLES ABERCROMBIE

Interludes and Poems	John Lane	1908
Mary and the Bramble *(out of print)*	The Author	1910
*The Sale of St. Thomas *(out of print)*	,,	1911
Emblems of Love	John Lane	1912
Deborah *(Play)*	,,	1912

GORDON BOTTOMLEY

The Crier by Night *(Play) (out of print)*	Unicorn Press	1902
The Gate of Smaragdus	Elkin Mathews	1904
Midsummer Eve *(Pastoral) (out of print)*	Peartree Press	1905
Chambers of Imagery I	Elkin Mathews	1907
The Riding to Lithend *(Play)*	Peartree Press	1909
Vision of Giorgione	T. B. Mosher, U.S.A.	1910
Chambers of Imagery II	Elkin Mathews	1912
King Lear's Wife	(in *Georgian Poetry 1913-1915*)	
Plays *(in preparation)*	Constable	

FRANCIS BRETT YOUNG

Five Degrees South	Martin Secker	1917
Poems 1916-1918	Collins	1919

WILLIAM H. DAVIES

The Soul's Destroyer	Alston Rivers	1906
New Poems	Elkin Mathews	1907
Nature Poems	A. C. Fifield	1908
Farewell to Poetry	,,	1910
Songs of Joy	,,	1911

* Reprinted in *Georgian Poetry 1911-1912.*

Foliage	Elkin Mathews	1913
The Bird of Paradise	Methuen	1914
Child Lovers	A. C. Fifield	1916
Collected Poems	,,	1916
*Raptures	Beaumont Press	1918
Forty New Poems	A. C. Fifield	1918

WALTER DE LA MARE

Poems	Murray	1906
The Listeners	Constable	1912
A Child's Day	,,	1912
Peacock Pie	,,	1913
Songs of Childhood (New Edition)	Longmans	1916
†The Sunken Garden	Beaumont Press	1917
Motley	Constable	1917
Collected Poems (*in preparation*) ,,		

JOHN DRINKWATER

Poems of Men and Hours	David Nutt	1911
Cophetua (*Play*)	,,	1911
Poems of Love and Earth	,,	1912
Cromwell	,,	1913
Rebellion (*Play*)	,,	1914
Swords and Ploughshares	Sidgwick & Jackson	1915
Olton Pools	,, ,,	1916
Poems, 1908-1914	,, ,,	1917
Pawns (*Plays*)	,, ,,	1917
Tides	Beaumont Press	1917
Tides (with additions)	Sidgwick & Jackson	1917
Loyalties	Beaumont Press	1918
,, (with additions)	Sidgwick & Jackson	1918
Lincoln (*prose play with Chorus*) ,, ,,		1918

* Reprinted with additional poems in *Forty New Poems*.
† Reprinted with additional poems in *Motley*.

JOHN FREEMAN

Twenty Poems	Gay & Hancock	1909
Fifty Poems (new edition)	Selwyn & Blount	1916
Stone Trees	,, ,,	1916
Presage of Victory	,, ,,	1916
Memories of Childhood	Morland Press	1918
,, and other Poems	Selwyn & Blount	1919

WILFRID WILSON GIBSON

Stonefolds	Elkin Mathews	1907
Akra the Slave	,, ,,	1910
Daily Bread	,, ,,	1910
Fires	,, ,,	1913
Borderlands	,, ,,	1914
Thoroughfares	,, ,,	1914
Battle	,, ,,	1915
Friends	,, ,,	1916
Livelihood	Macmillan	1917
Collected Poems	Macmillan Co., New York	1917
Whin	Macmillan	1918
Home	Beaumont Press	1919

ROBERT GRAVES

Over the Brazier	Poetry Bookshop	1916
Fairies and Fusiliers	Heinemann	1917
Country Sentiment	Secker	1919

D. H. LAWRENCE

Love Poems	Duckworth	1913
Amores	,,	1916
Look ! We Have Come Through !	Chatto & Windus	1917
New Poems	Martin Secker	1918

HAROLD MONRO

Judas	Sampson Low	1908
Before Dawn	Constable	1911

Children of Love	Poetry Bookshop	1914
Strange Meetings	,, ,,	1917

THOMAS MOULT   Contributions to *Voices*

1919

ROBERT NICHOLS

Invocation	Elkin Mathews	1915
Ardours and Endurances	Chatto & Windus	1917
The Budded Branch	Beaumont Press,	1918

SIEGFRIED SASSOON

The Old Huntsman	Heinemann	1917
Counter Attack	,,	1918
Picture Show (privately printed)	Cambridge University Press	1919
War Poems	Heinemann	1919

EDWARD SHANKS

Songs (*out of print*)	Poetry Bookshop	1915
Poems	Sidgwick & Jackson	1916
The Queen of China	Martin Secker	1919

FREDEGOND SHOVE

Dreams and Journeys	Blackwell	1919

J. C. SQUIRE

Imaginary Speeches (verse and prose)	Allen & Unwin	1912
Steps to Parnassus	Allen & Unwin	1913
The Survival of the Fittest	,, ,,	1916
Tricks of the Trade	Martin Secker	1917
. . . .
Poems : First Series	,, ,,	1918
The Birds and other Poems	,, ,,	1919

W. J. TURNER

The Hunter	Sidgwick & Jackson	1916
The Dark Fire	,, ,,	1918

Georgian Poetry (I)
1911—1912
Edited by E. M.

Pp. 197.   Thirteenth Thousand.
Brown Boards.

Price 6s. net (postage 4d).

Georgian Poetry (II)
1913—1915
Edited by E. M.

Pp. 244.   Twelfth Thousand.
Blue Boards.

Price 6s. net (postage 5d).

Georgian Poetry (III)
1916—1917
Edited by E. M.

Pp. 186.   Eleventh Thousand.
Green Boards.

Price 6s. net (postage 4d).

THE
POETRY BOOKSHOP

was founded in 1912 with the object of establishing a practical relation between poetry and the public.

READINGS OF POETRY

are given once or twice a week at six o'clock, except during July, August and September.

The charge for admission to Readings is at present Sixpence for each person. A programme is issued every month, which can be obtained at the Bookshop, or will be sent by post to any address at a charge of One Shilling a year. Single copies will be sent by post on receipt of a stamped envelope.

The FOLLOWING LISTS are sent post free on application :—

A List of some of the Principal Volumes of Modern Poetry stocked by the Poetry Bookshop.

A List of Books on Subjects connected with the Technique, History and Criticism of Poetry.

A List of Poetry Bookshop Publications.

When special information about poetry is wanted, a stamped envelope should be sent, and the nature of the particulars required should always be stated.

Although only Poetry, the Drama, and books connected with these subjects are kept in stock, publications of other kinds are promptly obtained to order.

Address :
35 DEVONSHIRE STREET, THEOBALDS ROAD, LONDON, W.C.1
PROPRIETOR : HAROLD MONRO.

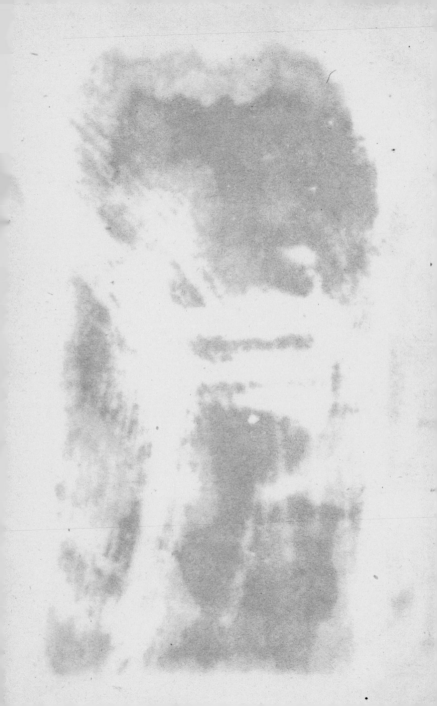